CURRICULUM IMPLEMENTATION AND INSTRUCTION: PEDAGOGICAL PERSPECTIVES

By

JEREMIAH, SAMUEL (Ph.D)

&

PROF. (MRS.) J. I. ALAMINA

i

CURRICULUM IMPLEMENTATION AND INSTRUCTION: PEDAGOGICAL PERSPECTIVES

Published by
Cel-Bez Publishing Co. (Nig.) Ltd.
#7 Kagha Street, Owerri, Nigeria
+2348035428158
E-mail: cel_bezpublishers@yahoo.com

First Published 2017
Copyright: **JEREMIAH, SAMUEL (Ph.D) &**
PROF. (MRS.) J. I. ALAMINA, 2017

ISBN: 978-978-045-754-9

Designed and Printed by
Cel-Bez Publishing Co. (Nig.) Ltd.
Owerri, Nigeria.

DEDICATION

This book is dedicated to all stakeholders involved in the process of curriculum implementation and instruction.

PREFACE

Curriculum studies is the heart beat of all educational programmes all over the world. This book titled Curriculum Implementation and Instruction: Pedagogical Perspectives focuses on critical areas that aim at exposing the readers to various conceptions and scope of a school curriculum.

The book therefore considers such curriculum issues as types of school curriculum, processes of developing a school curriculum, curriculum implementation and instruction.

Other areas considered are instructional methods, instructional materials and evaluating instructional outcomes. We believe that, the systematic approach used in anlysing the content area of this book, provides a soft landing for all readers, especially those involved on the process of curriculum implementation and instruction.

Jeremiah, S.

Alamina, J. I.

ACKNOWLEDGEMENT

We thank the various individuals, groups and organizations that contributed in diverse ways to the publication of this work.

We are particularly grateful to our professional colleagues and students. Our interactions with them provided some useful information that added to the successful completion of this work. We also appreciate authors whose works were consulted or even cited in this work. We also appreciate Mr. Ezekiel M. Amachree for his editoral contributions to this work. Above all, we give God all the glory.

Jeremiah, S.

Alamina, J. I.

FOREWORD

I have always likened the curriculum of any educational system to the heart in a human body. I am of the view that just as a man or woman with a weak heart cannot be expected to participate in an Olympic race or any other competitive race, so can we not expect a country with a weak and irrelevant curriculum to remain competitive in the community of nations.

Curriculum is often an elusive term to students in education. They do not fully appreciate its meaning and important and hence may rush to pursue programmes in Educational Planning and Management often with the false hope of becoming school administrators. Of course we know that to become a seasoned school administrator (Principal), one has to rise through the ranks as a teacher and must confront issues relating to the curriculum.

This book on Curriculum Implementation and Instruction is a veritable resource material to both staff and students of education. It is a book of eight (8) chapters that covers all aspects of Curriculum Development and Implementation. Chapter one explains the full meaning of curriculum and the other component of curriculum such as Programme of Studies, Programme of Activities, Academic Guidance, Vocational Guidance and Personal-Social Guidance. The chapter uses a graphic organizer to show the relationship among these components.

Chapter two dwells on the important topic on Patterns of Curriculum Organization. Different Curriculum designs/patterns are presented ranging from the Subject Matter pattern to the Broad-field or Integrated pattern, the various ramification of the Core pattern, Official and the Actual Curriculum, Informal or Hidden Curriculum, Teacher centered versus Learner centered curriculum. The advantages and disadvantages of each pattern is also presented.

Chapter three discusses the important topic on Process of Developing a School Curriculum. The chapter highlights the importance of goals and objectives and how to specify these. The other stages in this process include planning, development, tryout and revision, implementation and quality control. Significant stakeholders in curriculum development are discussed including over ten agencies that are actively involved in curriculum development at the different levels of education in Nigeria.

Chapter four is on Innovation and Change and covers such important topics as requirements for curriculum innovation and change, Factors that influence Curriculum Innovation and change and Innovation and Change Models are presented while chapter five is on the nitty-gitty of curriculum implementation encompassing syllabus, scheme of work, lesson plan and its parts including discussion of the Cambridge Teaching Knowledge Task (TKT) model and the Constructivist Based Model. Factors that hinder curriculum implementation are also highlighted.

Chapter six explores the various types of teaching methods while chapter seven is on types of Instructional materials. Chapter eight sums up the book with a detailed presentation on evaluation.

This textbook is a compendium of everything a student should know about curriculum. It should serve as a good reference material for teachers and training consultants who want to be current on what curriculum is all about and how to develop and implement it.

Prof. H.I. Dike
Faculty of Technical and Science Education
Department of Educational Foundations
Rivers State University
Nkpolu-Oroworukwu,
Port Harcourt, Rivers State, Nigeria

TABLE OF CONTENT

CHAPTER FIVE
CURRICULUM IMPLEMENTATION AND
INSTRUCTION   119

CHAPTER ONE

MEANING AND SCOPE OF A SCHOOL CURRICULUM

Introduction

The centre piece of this text is curriculum implementation, as such it becomes very vital to first of all examine the concept of curriculum as it will give the readers a firsthand information about the major issue at stake. Hence, this chapter takes a look at the meaning of curriculum as postulated by different scholars from the historical perspectives, narrow and broad points of view, to the contemporary era. The chapter will also discuss what constitutes a school curriculum by analyzing the scope of a curriculum such as, programme of studies, programme of Activities and programme of guidance. With these the stage is set for further discussions in the text.

Concept of Curriculum

Curriculum is one of the concepts that is mostly used when issues concerning the school are discussed. Such discussion may emerge from the lay man, politicians, concerned citizens, members of other professions and teachers alike. This is as a result of the importance of curriculum in the school system and the society at large. This issue is clearly stated in Etuk and Afangide (2008), as they spell out that among the many demands of a professional teacher is the knowledge of curriculum. In many teacher education programmes, curriculum is mandatory. The implication therefore is that anyone who wants to become a professional teacher must take a variety of courses in the area of curriculum.

Despite the importance of curriculum to the teacher and the society at large, it sounds very ironical to note that the concept of curriculum is one of the areas in the field of education that has posed a lot of problems in terms of definition. Danga as cited by Jeremiah (2004) notes that curriculum is one of the concepts in the field of education that has defied a single definition, there are many definitions of curriculum as there are authorities in the field. Gbamanja (2005) also averres that among all the myriad of components of education process, curriculum seems to be the most ambiguous and difficult to define. Gbamanja further points out that, this is so because curriculum reflects societal characteristics and trends. People therefore, tend to look at the curriculum based on their educational aims and objectives and how this could be executed and achieved. The difficulties in defining curriculum is further expressed by Oteh and Akuma (2010).

Historically, the term curriculum is derived from a Latin word "currus", which means race or to run a race. When properly interpreted, it means a relatively standardized ground to be covered by a learner on his race towards a finished line. Such finished line may be a school certificate, diploma or a degree depending on the programme. The implication of the above analysis is that the curriculum can be viewed as a racecourse. Immediately, the individual learner is admitted into the school, the race begins and stops at the end of the child's educational career. Currus, was used for a chaise, a horse-drawn carriage with a back-rest on two or four-wheels and used for pleasure or for carriage. It was used as a means of transportation in the ancient time. By the nineteenth century, the curriculum had come to be used in reference to education. It had certainly become an integral part of the educational circle where many now refer to it as a regular course of study or training in the school system.

Curriculum as a concept can also be viewed in two perspectives such as the narrow and the broad perspectives. Early definitions of curriculum looked at it from the narrow point of view. To them the curriculum was seen as the content area of individual subjects studied in the school which may be nursery, primary, secondary, university or any other formal or semi-formal segment of the school system. To this view Jeremiah and Alamina (2006) citing Maccia indicate that the curriculum is a presented instructional content. The definition of Robbit (1918), Todd (1965) and Johnson (1967) as cited by Oteh and Akuma (2010) all indicate, the narrow perspective of the school curriculum. The school curriculum cannot only be seen as the content area of different school subject, because there must be a close interaction between the Learner, subject and the entire school environment. Hence, this interaction process has a significant influence on the school curriculum. Relating the curriculum to the content area of school subject is only an aspect of the school curriculum which cannot produce an all-round learner. It was as a result of these criticisms and others that led to the broad concept of curriculum.

Those who look at curriculum on the broad perspective see it as all embracing, which means the totality of all the experiences learners have, under the auspices of the school. Bauchamp cited by Jeremiah andAlamina (2006) opines that the curriculum is the design of a social group for the educational experience of its members. Wheeler as noted by Biodum (2009) indicates that curriculum is the planned and guided learning experience brought to the learners under the auspices of the school. The definition of Wheeler may not be accepted mostly on the ground that he used the word "planned and guided". Curriculum may not be limited to only planned and guided activities. There are also other unplanned activities which the individual learner may encounter in the school that are also of a great importance to the overall development of the learner and the society at large. Hence, Tanner and Tanner (1975) explain that curriculum is the planned and guided learning experience and intended learning outcome formulated through the systematic reconstruction of knowledge and experience brought to the learner under the auspices of the school for the learners continued growth and contributions to the society. Terner's concept of curriculum, though accepted by many scholars, is faulted on the ground that it also used the words planned and "guided learning experience", as indicated earlier by D.K. Wheeler. Obanya as cited by Jeremiah (2010) explains that curriculum involves all the process taken to ensure that as the individual learner is passing through the school, the school is also passing through the learner. Obanya's view of curriculum has some flavour of professionalism. In this regard, the school is seen as a processing machine that processes the individual child into a finished product, quite different from the raw state it was before admission into the school. These changes help in the individuals contributions towards the development of the society. At this point, one can therefore say that a school curriculum is all the desirable learning experiences presented to the learner under the control of the school, for the learners personal growth and positive contributions towards the development of his society.

From the above analysis, a school curriculum can be divided into three components as noted by Biodum (2009) as follows.

Programme of Studies:

As hinted earlier, this aspect of curriculum is the oldest. It is associated with the traditional idea of *course of study*. Traditionally, curriculum was regarded as narrowly concerned with the promotion of 'knowledge acquisition' or 'impartation of knowledge'. For example, Olarinoye (2001) adopts this narrow perspective in defining curriculum as blueprint consisting of subject themes, topics performance or behavioural objectives, content or subject matter and students' activities. The emphasis here is on knowledge. Such knowledge is to be derived from the accumulated experiences and wisdom of the society for which the curriculum is meant to serve. This narrow concern on covering specific subject content has little or no room for other activities outside the content spelt out in the syllabus. At best, such other activities are described as *extra-curricular*.

The idea of 'programme of studies' is largelyto guide the process of developing the teaching-learning activities. The content materials for these activities are selected basic ideas, concepts, principles and generalizations central to the effective development of the learner and his or her society. In the narrow sense, such concerns could focus on the content of individual subjects such as Geography, History, Social Studies, Integrated Science or Economics. On the other hand, attention might be broadened to focus on groups of subjects. It is in this latter sense that the *National Policy on Education* (Federal Republic of Nigeria, 2004) groups certain areas of secondary school learning as 'Core Subjects' while some others are grouped as 'Electives' and yet others as 'Optional'. Whether in the narrow or broad sense of it, it is important to note that a programme or studies is usually about what content should be emphasized in the day-to-day operations of the school system. Beyond knowledge acquisition, however, the learner needs to be developed in some other areas of life so as to be useful to him or herself, and make meaningful contributions to the development of his or her society. So, the curriculum developer must equally emphasise domains that go beyond mere knowledge acquisition to cover those of values, appreciations, competencies and so on. To fully achieve this demands paying adequate attention to the other components of the curriculum.

Programme of activities:

This aspect of the school life essentially covers those areas of life, domains of influence and platforms of interactions that were traditionally called *extra-curricular*, *extra-class* or *co-curricular* activities. Such activities are usually not written in the strict sense of subject content. However, they constitute vital areas of knowledge enrichment of immeasurable value. For instance, many documented activities and events which otherwise would have been 'studies' in textbooks could be practically observed through visits to the activity sites. Maximum benefits are derived through such activites which could come in form of field research, field teaching or excursion. *Field research* involves going out to collect some data about the activities and events of interests and such data are later processed during classroom teacing. In the case of *field teaching*, the resource persons at the sites visited do the bulk of the teaching and the regular teacher merely makes occasional contributions where and when necessary. Excursion largely involves more relaxed field activities than either field research or field teaching.

The three put together however, provide windows of additional insights and perspectives that rigid content specification may be incapable of providing. Beside these sources of activities, students could also derive a lot of benefits from their participation in voluntary organizations and associations such as Boys Scout, Girl's Guid, AIDS Awareness Club, Literary and Debating Society, and the Junior Engineers, Technicians and Scientists (JETS) Club. Activities of these various clubs stand to teach several lessons in selfeless service, value development and skill acquisition that go far beyond what the routine of an inflexible 'programme of studies' and school time-table could ever provide. For example, membership of the AIDS Awareness Club could provide a platform for secondary school adolescents to become *change-champions* in influencing the risky lifestyles of their peers and siblings in both the short and long terms. Such involvement brings personal and social benefits to the students. First, the students become more knowledgeable about the causes and ways of transmitting the disease and this could equip them in protecting themselves against contacting HIV which matures to AIDS. Secondly, their involvement in such awareness campaigns helps to equip them right from early in life with skills for working for the promotion of healthier society for the benefit of all. To derive maximum benefits from both the academic and co-curricular activities of the school, however, there is need for proper guidance.

Programme of Guidance:

By guidance, we mean the support given by the school to enable learners derive maximum benefits from learning activities based on interests, abilities, aspirations and other attributes that are personal to them. In the contemporary school situation, the term 'guidance' is always used with reference to 'counselling'. The latter concept deals with the process of assisting the individual to become a personal problem-solver. While guidance is about lending support to identify options; counselling takes it to a higher level of weighing the identified options to ensure that the client takes an informed decision on a particular matter of interest. In essence, the programme of guidance provides avenues for learners to fully harness their potentials by engaging in activities that are most meaningful, challenging and rewarding in both the immediate sense as well as in the foreseeable future. Such support services could be distilled into three: vocational guidance, educational guidance, and personal-social guidance (Emeruwa, 1998).

Vocational guidance: Of the three broad areas of guidance and counseling services, vocational guidance is the oldest. Indeed, early definitions of guidance tended to limit it to providing support on career opportunities in the learning of school subjects. This, perhaps, was part of efforts to distinguish the task of guidance and counseling from that of general education which is to produce a complete person. While it may be relevant to secondary education in our environment, such perspective to vocational guidance may however not be too helpful at the primary schools level because those involved are still in their formative years. In the public primary schools, guidance and counseling services are not provided separate from the classroom teaching. Rather, they are integrated into the day-to-day activities of teachers. At the secondary level, however, guidance and counseling services are gaining increasing popularity.

From the curriculum point of view, however, it should be noted that vocational guidance is an integral part of the teacher's professional calling – be it under the programme of studies or that of activities. For instance, a good class teacher should be able to identify each of his or her students' interests in various school subjects and suggest possible career pathways as they advance towards the end of their secondary education. Through participation in literary and debating activities, for example; it is possible to identify those who may want to pursue a career in law or literary studies.

Students who consistently do the school proud in science-oriented competitions like the JETS could also be encouraged towards making careers in the engineering, medicine and other science-oriented fields. The point being stressed here is that the teacher, as a curriculum developer, must be conscious of how both programmes of studies and activities coalesce into giving their learners career options. But where difficulties still arise about what career path a particular student is to follow, the teacher certainly requires the services of a professional career/vocational counsellor.

Education guidance: The goal of sending every child to school is to profit maximally from learning and become the best human that he or she is capable of becoming. Educational guidance aims at attaining this goal by focusing on school achievement. Where learners have difficulties, intervention programmes such as remedial and/or rehabilitative counseling, are required. In addition, educational counseling assists in the choice of school subjects especially at the upper level of secondary education to serve as the basis for vocational guidance. Such guidance services are however closely tied to individual learners' interests, abilities and future aspirations.

Like in vocational guidance, every subject teacher has a role to play in the early detection of learning difficulties among the students they teach. This is especially so in the primary and junior secondary education levels under the nine-year compulsory schooling introduced with the implementation of the

11

Universal Basic Education (UBE) scheme. At these levels, all school subjects are compulsory and the early detection of learning difficulties might reduce the degree of frustration and disenchantment that characterize the behaviours of underacheivers in schools. It is obvious that frustrated and disenchanted learners can hardly derive maximum benefits from their participation in schooling – whether at the primary, secondary or tertiary level of education.

Personal-social guidance: Beside guiding learners towards some career paths and helping to reduce difficulties along their way, guidance services are also provided to address the challenges they face in developing their total person. Some learners are nervous or shy to make presentation in class. Others suffer sundry impairments such as speech disorder, introversion, extroversion and reclusion that make them feel uncomfortable working within groups. Early detection of these and other inhibitors to learning allows for intervention before they constitute serious impediments. This is because, while students may learn beautiful ideas about the qualities of a good citizen from their teacher, it is among their peers and other significant groups that the practice of good citizenship begins. Applied to the curriculum field, it is clear that a learner is not fully developed if he or she does not know where to look for solution when in difficulty or relate well in the midst of others. Such a situation calls for taking another look at the school's programmes of studies and activities.

COMPONENT OF A SCHOOL CURRICULUM

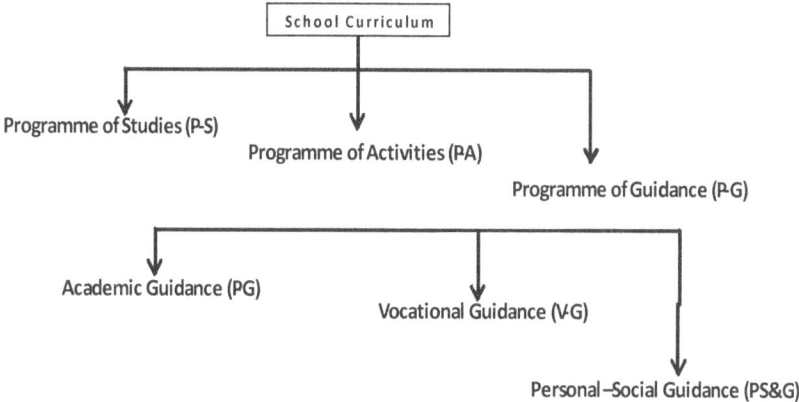

Figure 1. Components of a school commission

Summary
In this first chapter we have been able to examine the concept of curriculum from the historical point of view, narrow and broadperspective. The chapter, in stating the problems inherent in the definition of curriculum also identified three major components of a comprehensive school curriculum by stating in clear terms the Interrelationship between these components in providing all round development of the learner. The chapter therefore concludes that though we may not have a universally acceptable definition of curriculum, but what constitute a school curriculum may be planned or unplanned learning experience directed towards the

13

development of the full potential of the learner and positive contribution towards the development of the society.

CHAPTER TWO

TYPES OF SCHOOL CURRICULUM

Introduction
In our previous chapter we examined the meaning of curriculum and its components. This provided a road map for further clarification on issues of curriculum implementation and instruction. Such issue can further be clarified by analyzing the various types of curriculum operating in our school. To this view therefore, this chapter examine among others types of curriculum based on design, official recognition and teacher-learner perspectives. Such arrangement provides an acceptable framework in discussing issues on curriculum implementation and instruction.

Types of School Curriculum
Experts in curriculum studies and other related areas have over the years identified a number or types of curriculum. These are based on pattern of curriculum organization as may be referred to by some other experts. Analyses of these types of curriculum are as follows:

Types of School Curriculum Based on Design
The major types of curriculum we will consider based on design include subject centered curriculum, broad field or integrated curriculum and core curriculum.

Subject-centred Curriculum:

Many curriculum experts such as Gbamanja (2005), Jeremiah and Alamina (2006), Offorma (1994), Mkpa and Izuagba (2012) believe that the subject- centred curriculum is the oldest form of curriculum to be implemented in the school system. According to Jeremiah and Alamina, the subject-centred curriculum dates its origin to the Greco-Roman era where the triuvium and Quadrivium dominated the curriculum. According to Mkpa (1987), Oteh and Akuma (2010), the triuvium means three things which consist of Grammar, Rhetoric, and Dialectics, while the quadrivium means four things which comprise Arithmetic, Geometry, Astronomy and Music. These subjects dominated the medieval schools and later the monasteries and cathedral schools. After so many years of existence these subjects were sub-divided into many disciplines or subject areas. In Nigeria for examples at the primary and secondary school level separate subjects such as Mathematics, English Language, Geography, History, Biology, Chemistry, Economics, Government, Physics and Agricultural Science are offered. Some of these subject areas are sub-divided into discrete areas for in-depth study. Mathematics for example is subdivided into Quantitative Reasoning, Arithmetic, Algebra, Geometry and Calculus to mention but a few. In English Language we have verbal reasoning, Essay, Comprehension, Lexis and Structure, etc.

Hence the subject-centred curriculum exists in a situation whereby the school programme is organized into a variable number of subjects, each of which purported represents a specialized body of knowledge. This is because each subject forms a compartmentalized aspect which represents a body of knowledge. In the subject-centred curriculum, mastery of the subject matter is usually the basis through which educational outcome are achieved. Another important issue about the subject-centred curriculum is that the subjects are taught in hierarchical order. The degree of importance accorded to any subject varies from one nation to another or socio-economic priorities. In Nigeria, during the colonial era, subjects such as history, literature and economics dominated the school system, than 'mathematics, physics, chemistry and biology. This was because at this era, the aim of education was to produce highly motivated civil servants who will mount the administrative position in Nigeria after independence. At present, the trend has changed. Science and technology education has taken over the school curriculum for scientific and technological advancement.

Advantages of the Subject-centred Curriculum

❖ Subject-centred Curriculum enhances easy assessment of instructional outcome. Instructional outcome in this regard can be measured using instrument such as teacher-made test and standardized test. The various single subjects offered in our school system today makes it possible for the use of standardized test such as West African School Certificate Examination, National Examination Council and Unified Tertiary Matriculation Examination (UTME) in assessing students achievement.

❖ Textbooks are more available and better organized under the Subject- centred Curriculum. Such texts are written by experts knowledgeable in the various field of study for the proper consumption of the learners. Such books are easily available for students and teachers in aiding the teaching learning process.

❖ Teachers are more conversant to implement the Subject-centred Curriculum than any other type in the school system. This is because the teachers are made to teach the subjects of their choice based on their areas of specialization and interest. Such subjects a taught using various strategies in which the teacher is trained for. The teacher also has the knowledge of planning his lesson for the overall benefit of the learner. This help to develop a high spirit of confidence, interest, motivation and satisfaction on both learners and teachers.

❖ Research work and in-depth specialization are better facilitated under the Subject-centred

Curriculum than any other type of curriculum. It is easier to conduct research work in Chemistry, Biology or Physics than Integrated Science which is a unique example of integrated curriculum. Such research work and in-depth knowledge enhances students achievement and retention.

❖ The Subject-centered Curriculum is more popular to implement in the school system than any other type of curriculum. Learners, parents and the general public are more conversant with the Subject Centered Curriculum. With this type of curriculum the progress of learners and the school in general can be more easily determined. The community is aware of the content, skill and attitude offered to the children from the various subjects. With such knowledge, community can contribute effectively towards improvement of the curriculum and the school in general.

Disadvantages of the Subject Centered Curriculum

❖ A major curriculum planning is the adoption of integration of curriculum in selecting content area with the view that different subjects are properly interrelated and brought to bear on social living. The Subject-centered Curriculum does not adopt this principle, the result is inadequate mental or intellectual development of learners as well as their ability to effectively relate this learning to society.

❖ The Subject-centered Curriculum is not learner centered. This is because little or no recognition is given to the problems, felt needs and interest of the learner. Its emphasis is on isolated subjects given greater recognition to the subject specialist than the individual learners. The teacher in any teaching learning process need to consider the learners background, experience and other related variables, but the Subject-centered Curriculum tend to play down on this ideal situation.

❖ Subject-centered Curriculum tends to isolate the content and experience from the real world of the learners. Specialization and research in Subject-centered Curriculum are often unrelated to what the learner experiences in his daily experience as a member of the society. On the contrary, the curriculum content of integrated discipline such as social studies, integrate science and introductory technology are often within the range of learners' day to day experiences.

❖ The Subject-centered Curriculum lays more or greater emphasis on examination as a major instrument of assessing and evaluating learners' instructional outcome. Such emphasis on examination, causes a lot of problem on the learners and the entire educational system. In order to pass such examination, most students and teachers tend to neglect other more important learning outcome such as problem solving ability and acquisition of social value. They prefer to focus more on cognitive knowledge necessary for passing such examination.

❖ Another significant setback of the Subject Centered Curriculum is the issue of proliferation of subjects. Proliferation in this regard means increase in the number of subjects. When the school timetable may not be able to accommodate all the subjects or allow adequate time for their study. In another view, when too many subjects are studied without one relating to another the learner is unlikely to enjoy a coherent education out of the whole lot.

Broad Field or Integrated Curriculum:
The Broad Field Curriculum emerged of a result of the various criticisms levied against the Subject-centered Curriculum. It aims at integrating, rather than diversifying the curriculum content. It brings different subject areas to integrate them into a whole for the learner to see the relationship between them. In a more simple understanding, integrated curriculum exist in a situation whereby two or more subject areas are fused together to form as single subject. In doing this, different approaches such as thematic, content-related and infused approaches are adopted. The philosophy behind curriculum integration is that there is an interrelationship of

knowledge (unity of knowledge) and that the learner learns better when issues are presented as a complex whole. In our contemporary school system, we have different examples of integrated subjects. At the primary school level, we have integrated subjects such as Social Studies, Civic Education, Basic Science and Cultural and Creative Arts. At the secondary level we have subjects such as Social Studies, Integrated Science, Business Studies, Introductory Technology, etc. All these subjects draw their content, scope and methodology from the traditional subjects using the above stated approaches.

Advantages of Broad Field or Integrated Curriculum

❖ The nature and scope of the Broad Field Curriculum can be described as the synthesis of different subjects. This is because the curriculum brings together hitherto separate subjects into a unified whole. Such designs help the learner to see a relationship among different subject areas.

❖ The pattern of organization in curriculum integration enhances positive transfer of knowledge. In curriculum integration, the subject matter so integrated cuts across various subject areas. In this situation, the learner can utilize ideas obtained from one subject area to understand more clearly, ideas in another subject area. In a similar development, when subject matters from some areas are integrated, the learner can draw experiences from a wider range of subject matters which could be brought to bear on a number of day to day situation.

❖ The Broad Field Curriculum offers greater coverage of the content than the subject-centred curriculum. This is because the selection of content and subject matter draw ideas from different subject areas. This idea makes the learners to have or gain knowledge related to other subject areas. In a practical example one lesson period spent can also be utilized to discuss topics in integrated science that are likely to cover the same topic discussed in physics.

❖ Another important advantage of the Broad Field Curriculum is that it is economical in terms of manpower or materials relative to its implementation process. For example in most critical situation a specialist in social studies may be engaged to teach government and other related discipline. Also instructional materials used in teaching integrated science, social studies, business studies or introductory technology may be utilized in the teaching of other related subjects.

❖ Broad Field Curriculum can be applied to all levels of our educational system ranging from the pre-primary, primary, secondary and tertiary levels. At the primary and secondary schools level, it enhances unity of knowledge as it will not lead to much confusion associated with excessive fragmentation as obtained in the subject-centred curriculum.

Disadvantages of Broad Field or Integrated Curriculum
- ❖ The resources for effective implementation of Broad Field or Integrated Curriculum may be difficult to obtain especially, if a topic in one integrated discipline cuts across about four or more subject areas.
- ❖ In actual fact, the potential for curriculum integration in the school system is limited. There are some subject areas that are very difficult to integrate because of their nature in terms of logical consideration. For example, there is little or no integration between Physics and Christian Religious Knowledge or Chemistry and Literature.
- ❖ Another important problem of curriculum integration is that it suffers the problem of lack of relevant textbooks that actually have the true flavour of curriculum integration. Most authors are trained to produce books in the various single subject areas. As a result when they attempt to write for subject in integrated discipline, their style often fail to affect the desired integration adequately.

❖ In another view, teachers are not properly trained professionally to implement the integrated curriculum in our school system. Most teachers in the Nigerian school system are trained in the traditional single subject areas, as such are incompetent to implement the integrated curriculum. This justifies the reason why most science and social science teachers in the school system have a wrong conception of subjects such as integrated science and social studies.

Core Curriculum:

Core is a Latin word meaning heart. This underscores the importance of this type of curriculum in the school system. Hence, Core Curriculum consists of those parts of learning experiences or learning process required by all students at a particular level of education as a result of their importance in the overall achievement of the objectives of education. In most societies, the Core Curriculum is held as a legitimate part of the government policy. In the United State of America for example, the Core Curriculum is designed to develop values and rules essential to social living. The approach in this regard is to study problem of broad society and to gather information from any source to aid in seeking solution. Core Curriculum does not focus on one discipline or subject area at a time, but attempts to integrate materials from various disciplines to accomplish the goal of the society. Some good examples of Core Curriculum are

English Language and Mathematics that are made compulsory courses in Secondary schools. It is also a separate course every learner must take as requirement for certification. At the university level certain courses within the framework of General Studies can also be regarded as Core Component of the programme. At the Teacher Education level, courses- such as History of Education, Curriculum Studies, Educational Psychology among others are also vital in the attainment of the objectives of teacher education. Hence, they can be regarded as Core Component of the teacher education programme. At the secondary school level, moral instruction, social studies and recently civic education also serves as Core Curriculum in the sense that they inculcate in our youths, moral values vital for harmonious existence of the society Taba (1962) explains that this type of curriculum should be designed to develop integration, to serve the needs of the learner and to promote active learning and significant relationship between life and learning. Zais (1976), Mkpa (1987), Jeremiah and Alamina (2006) all identify six types of core curriculum that can be implemented in the school system. These are:

Separate Subject Core:
These refer to the separate subjects that are treated as core component of the school programme. As a result of their importance, they are considered very useful and important to students at a particular level. In Nigeria for example the National Policy on

Education (2004) considers English Language, French, Mathematics, Integrated Science, Social Studies, Introductory Technology and one Nigerian language as core curriculum at the junior secondary school level. At the senior secondary, the core curriculum include English Language, Mathematics, one of (Biology, Chemistry, Physics or Science) one of (Literature, History, Geography or Religious Studies) and a vocational subject. At the primary school level, the entire subjects in the school curriculum serve as core because it is the foundation for the future education.

Correlated Core:
This type of core is an attempt to correlate two or more separate core subject to provide knowledge vital for the development of the learner. For example, in an essay competition, a teacher might ask the student to write or discuss a topic on Economics or even science. In such an attempt, two subjects, English, Science or even Economics can be correlated. In another type of core, the subject matters of a core subject are selected and organized with reference to broad name of the core concerned. For example, Government or Political Science and Economics may be correlated in a theme such as the place of leadership in the development of Nigerian economy. At the Nigeria Certificate of Education (NCE) level, general studies course such as "Political Economy" is a unique example of correlated core.

Fused core:
In this type of core curriculum a number of subjects are unified or integrated into a core subject. In more simple terms, the fused core has a stylistic resemblance with the integrated curriculum. For example, in Social Studies, we have integration of subjects such as Sociology, History, Economics, Geography and Anthropology. Also in Integrated Science, we have the Fusion of Chemistry, Biology, Physics and Health Science. Citizenship Education as studied as a GSE course at the NCE level is also a unique example of fused core.

Activities Experienced core:
This is a type of programme of general education which is child-centred in the sense that it focuses on learning associated with felt need and interest of the learner. It shares similar characteristics with the activities or experience centred curriculum the activities in this type of curriculum are cooperatively taken by teachers and learners. Local Craft or Home Craft, Cultural and Creative Arts are good examples of the activities or experience core. Others may include game and sports, field trip and other organized activities of the school system.

Area of Living Core:
The main idea of area of living component of core curriculum is that it is pre-planned to provide general education based on social problem. Hence, it adopts the problem solving model in its implementation process. In area of living core, ideas

may be borrowed from separate subjects with a view of devising appropriate means of addressing those problems. Example of such problems in Nigeria may include food scarcity occasioned by low productivity in agriculture, ecological problems such as soil erosion, flooding and desertification.

Social problem Core:
The social problem core, like the area of living core focuses on the society, but differs from it in that, the area of living core is based on "such universal and uncontroversial human activities, the social problem core examines the crucial and controversial issues in the contemporary society". Examples of such issues include women in politics, girl child or boy child education; others may include, religious conflicts, Niger Delta struggle, military issue, resource control. In Nigeria today, the issue of youth restiveness and ethnic conflicts have paved way for the emergence of the course Peace and conflict studies offered as a general studies in institutions of Higher Learning.

Advantages of Core Curriculum
- ❖ The core curriculum can be used for proper guidance and counselling of the learner by the teacher and other stakeholders in the school system. As they come together to plan and implement the core programme, teachers easily identify students' problem areas and proffer adequate solutions.

❖ The core curriculum also shares the advantages of integrated curriculum mostly the fused and correlated core. These aspects of core curriculum tend to reconcile aspects of distinct subjects into a unity for the learners proper understanding and appreciation of essential relationship of the subject.

❖ Core curriculum prepares the learner better for life in the wider society as does the integrated curriculum. The core curriculum objectives are broader in scope and more comprehensive in nature than those of the subject-centred curriculum.

❖ Core curriculum deals with societal problems, needs and aspiration of the learner. The learners are able to associate what they have learnt in the school with life outside the school thereby making learning more meaningful to the learners.

❖ More importantly, learning experiences are employed by the core programme because the learners are often involved in the planning of some of the variables of the core most especially the activities core. Their participation offers more than the desired opportunity to suggest activities of their choice. Hence the core curriculum is learner friendly in nature.

Disadvantages of Core Curriculum
❖ The objectives of core curriculum may deviate significantly from those of the subject centered

curriculum. This may make the learner loose interest as they may not have the desired need of studying them.

❖ The content of core curriculum in many cases are drawn from the society, and societal problems. In a heterogeneous society such as ours, this type of curriculum may not be uniformly applicable even to the learners at the same level.

❖ Another issue concerning the problem of core curriculum is lack of textbooks and other resource material required for effective teaching and learning of the content. Since social problems continue to change from place to place, no standard textbook can stand the test of time to meet the demand of the content area of the curriculum.

❖ In Nigeria and other developing countries of the world, most teachers are not trained in the proper implementation of the core curriculum. In this regard, it implies that the core curriculum is not as popular as the subject-centred curriculum.

❖ Core curriculum does not lead to specialization on the part of the learner, which is a characteristic of the subject centered curriculum.

In the presence of the subject centred curriculum which emphasizes high specialization, the core curriculum become more unpopular and inferior in producing the needed manpower in a globalized economy.

Type of Curriculum based on Official Recognition

The various types of curriculum that fall under this category include official and actual curriculum and informal or hidden curriculum.

Official and Actual Curriculum:

This form of curriculum refers to the actual content of the school programme that is documented in the school syllabus, prospectus or minimum standard as the case may be. In actual fact, it is the programme of studies component of the school curriculum. One important issue about the official curriculum is that it is provided by examination bodies or administrative machineries responsible for the affairs of education at a given level. In some situations, official curriculum may be central or decentralized utilizing various model for its implementation process in Nigeria for example, official curriculum for primary school is provided by the National Educational Research and Development Council in conjunction with the Universal Basic Education Commission. At the secondary school levels, such is provided by the Federal Ministry of Education and the various examination bodies such as the West African Examination Council, National Examination Council and the Joint Admission Matriculation Board. The Colleges of Education Official Curriculum is designed by National

Commission for Colleges of Education while those of Universities are drawn by National Universities Commission.

Actual Curriculum:
When the official curriculum gets into thevarious schools, it becomes the responsibility of the school authority and the teachers to draw out a scheme of work for each subject mostly at the primary and secondary school level. In the course of drawing out the scheme, some modifications or adjustments can be made to suit the local condition. After this level, the teacher draws out a lesson plan for each topic identified in the scheme of work and presents it to the students in the class. Thus one can say that the actual curriculum is what takes place in the class. It is the implementation stage of the official curriculum which involves the "classroom" effort of the teacher, students and other stakeholders in putting into operation or practice what is obtained in the curriculum document. The teacher in this regard plays a major role. This may justify the reason why the National Policy on Education (2004) spelt out that "no Nation can rise above the quality of its teachers".

Advantages of Official and Actual Curriculum
  ❖ The official curriculum gives direction to the learners on what they are expected to learn at a particular level and time. The official curriculum outlines the topics to be covered by the students and teachers alike. Knowledge

of such topics can lead to independent learning on the part of the learner. Such can enhance achievement.

❖ The actual curriculum gives the teacher the opportunity to make some input to the process of curriculum development and implementation. This is because at this stage, the teacher has the professional right to modify the curriculum to suit local needs.

❖ Through this type of curriculum, evaluation of instructional outcome become easier. Teachers will be more aware about what they have taught and the learners what they have learnt. Through this, self appraisal of teachers, performance can be easily measured.

❖ The official and actual curriculum affords the various stakeholders in curriculum development process the opportunity to contribute their expert skills to the process of curriculum development and implementation. Such stakeholders include curriculum bodies, teachers, learners and the society. This approach makes the curriculum to have both learner-centred and society centred flavour.

Disadvantages of Official and Actual Curriculum
❖ The curriculum content of the official and actual curriculum may be misinterpreted by the presence of untrained teacher who may not have the pedagogical knowledge of drawing out a scheme from the official

curriculum or the methodology of explaining the instructional content.

❖ In Nigeria and other developing nations of the world, poor school environment as characterized in our school system may hinder the implementation of this type of curriculum.

❖ The official curriculum also suffers a major deficiency of depending too much on the content area of the curriculum to the detriment of other school activities or experiences that may also be important to the learner. Its main focus is on the development of cognitive domain which prepares the learners for the various examinations without much emphasis on the affective and psychomotor domains.

Hidden Curriculum

The hidden curriculum consists of those aspects of knowledge which the child acquires in the school but is not consciously built into the official curriculum. As the individual learner involves himself in the various academic programmes of the school or programme of study, there is that tendency that such a learner must also encounter certain experiences that may enable him function better in the programme of studies. Such activities though are not outline in the school syllabus, contribute positively towards attainment of educational goal. Such learning experiences can be referred to as hidden curriculum. Examples are gender role, dignity of Larbour, respect for constituted authority, Jeremiah and Alamina (2006) note that hidden curriculum in most cases is based on the cultural background of the learner or the prevailing cultural setting of the immediate environment. They further state that children mostly at the primary and junior secondary school levels learn most of these activities and value system by imitation and observation, hence, the teacher can only inculcate these values by being a good role model for the pupils to imitate.

Advantages of Hidden Curriculum
- ❖ Hidden curriculum can be used to promote the rich cultural heritage of the society.
- ❖ The implementation of the curriculum is not so complex. Textbooks, classrooms or other instructional materials may not be a vital tool for its implementation.
- ❖ The curriculum does not need much expert knowledge of the teacher for its implementation.
- ❖ The curriculum can be used to inculcate good moral and social values to the learners.

Disadvantages of Hidden Curriculum
- ❖ Since the hidden curriculum is not documented, it cannot be universally applied in a heterogeneous society such as ours. In a similar view, it can also fade with time.

* Variables such as cultural pattern of the people, and gender may affect the actual implementation of the curriculum.
* The hidden curriculum does not aim at any terminal examination or assessment instrument. In this situation, students, teachers, and even the general public may show lack of confidence on the hidden curriculum.

Types of Curriculum based on Teacher-Learner Perspectives

The major types of curriculum to be examined under this sub-heading include the teacher-centred and learner centered curriculum.

Teacher Centred Curriculum

The teacher-centred curriculum is an old concept in curriculum literature. Its origin is traced to the ancient educational system of and Greece where the teacher dominates the instructional process with little or no consideration for the learners. The teacher-centred curriculum sees the teacher's role principally as that of director of knowledge and works on the assumption that in all, learning situations, the teacher's role is superior and above all, he knows the best. Farrant (1987), postulates that the teacher- centred curriculum focuses on what is to be taught rather than the child who is taught, so that education is seen more as working through the syllabus than as trying to help each learner develop his inherent potentials. In this curriculum, emphasis is on teaching rather than learning.

Some major characteristics of the teacher-centred curriculum are as follows:

* Teachers acts as essential link between the child and what he is learning.
* Teacher selects what the child learns methods by which he will learn and the pace at which he learns.
* Teacher sees their role as communicating knowledge to their pupils as efficiently as possible.
* Teacher spends most of their time actually teaching.
* Pupils get the impression that they can only learn when their teacher is present and teaching.
* Pupils tend to be regarded as more or less uniform groups of learner rather than as individuals with different gift and needs.

Advantages of Teacher-centred Curriculum

* The teacher-centred curriculum is more popular in our school system, than the learner centered curriculum. This is because our school system are more trained in the implementation of this type of curriculum.

* In the teacher-centred curriculum, more emphasis is placed on the curriculum content rather than the child's activities. This makes

the child to be more equipped and prepared for external assessment procedure.

❖ The implementation process of the teacher-centred curriculum is not as complex as those of the learner-centred curriculum. This is because the teacher-centred curriculum may not need much material for its implementation.

❖ The teacher-centred curriculum is not only limited to the pre-primary school levels as in the case of some other types of curriculum. It can be adopted favourably in primary, secondary and the tertiary levels.

❖ Since the curriculum requires greater pre-planning on the part of the teacher for effective implementation, it gives the teacher opportunity to have a better insight into the curriculum.

Disadvantages of Teacher-centred Curriculum

❖ In the teacher-centred curriculum, the teacher dictates what the learner should learn. In this situation, the curriculum does not give learners any opportunity to have active participation in the learning, process.

❖ The teacher-centred curriculum does not take into consideration the principles of individual differences. The learners in this regard are considered as more or less uniform group of learners rather than individuals having different needs and aspirations.

❖ Another major criticism of the teacher-centred curriculum is what it tends to focus mainly on the cognitive aspect of knowledge to a great disadvantage of effective aspect of knowledge. This may lead to rote learning.

❖ The teacher-centred curriculum tends to widen the relationship between the teacher and the learners in the teaching/learning process. This is because the teacher only dictates the content of instruction to be presented to the learner. The teacher sees himself as having absolute knowledge to impart rather than facilitate the needed learning. On the other hard, the learner perceives himself as a receptor whose knowledge depends only on the teacher. In any ideal learning situation, there must be a mutual cooperation between the learner and the teacher.

Learner-centred Curriculum

The learner or child-centred curriculum emerged as a result of the various criticisms levelled at the teacher centered curriculum. The major focus of the child-centred curriculum is the interest and the active participation of the learner in the teaching/learning process. This design is structured with the learners felt needs and interest in mind. The child-centred curriculum has both philosophical and psychological undertone in its design. On the psychological point of view, the child-centred curriculum is based on the importance of learners' involvement in activities of the teaching learning process. The philosophical consideration of the curriculum are progressivism and pragmatism. These two school of thought stress the importance of the learner and activities in any learning engagement.

For the teacher to actually apply the child-centred curriculum, his major concern should include the discovery of learners interest and more importantly assist the learners in the selection of the most important one for study. In this situation therefore, the curriculum calls for an extensive planning by the teacher before it can be successfully implemented. The teacher must assist the learners to make decision on what to do, how to do it, and above all be involved in the process of evaluation. This implies that there is a high degree of cooperation between the teacher and the learner in the child-centred curriculum. The child-centred curriculum adopts the problem-solving method. On the process of exerting the learning based on the interest of the learner, a properly planned programme of studies should present the learner with definite problem, which they should grapple with. As they succeed in solving the said problem, they not only find answers to puzzling situation but more importantly, they acquire important skills in responsibility, group work, meaningful planning and execution of projects as well as limitations. On the preparation towards the successful implementation of this type of curriculum, the teacher need not involve himself so much on strict planning in advance. This is because the learner's interest, needs and mode of learning determine how learning takes place. Much pre-planning will alter precise knowledge of the learners interest at any given point in time.

A wide range of course or subjects should be offered to the learner so that each learner should engage in what best meet his interest or needs. This said learning should be problem-centred in addition, a variety of opportunities and activities should be provided so that the various interest of the learner will be accommodated.

Advantages of Child Centred Curriculum
- ❖ The teaching/learning process centres on the activities and experience of the child. For this reason, learning becomes more meaningful and purposeful to the learners. The learner is better motivated to learn because what they are learning is an outcome of their desire rather than a teacher-prescribed content. The outcome of this is the reality and meaningfulness of what is learned.
- ❖ The child-centred curriculum focuses on individual differences of the learner. When different learning opportunities are provided, each learner fits into particular activity that suits his interest and felt needs.
- ❖ The child-centred curriculum also utilizes problem solving models which are vital in

42

contemporary teaching/learning engagement. One major purpose of any meaningful programme of learning is the development of skills which can be applied in other problem solving situations.

Disadvantages of Child Centered Curriculum
- ❖ The design lays much emphasis on activities than the subject matter. This fact makes the design limited in its capacity to provide all round education to the learner. It aim more on the development of affective and psychomotor domain to the detriment of cognitive aspect of knowledge.
- ❖ The child who is acquainted with this type of curriculum is not likely to adjust successfully to the type of subject curriculum he will eventually encounter in the secondary or tertiary level. The examination which learners face in the higher institution demand that they should have passed through the subject curriculum. In this situation, the child-centred curriculum tends to alienate the learner from successful subject design in his future education.
- ❖ The possibility of implementing the child-centred curriculum may be limited to the pre-primary school level. This is because the primary and secondary school levels are geared towards some examination with a

definite syllabus provided by assessment bodies.

❖ Another major setback of the child-centred curriculum is that it needs a lot of materials in the form of textbooks, pupils' guide, teachers' guide and even play materials. In Nigeria, only a few well established private schools can afford to provide such materials to the learners and the teachers. This implies that implementation of such curriculum depends highly on availability of finance for the provision of such materials.

❖ This type of curriculum is not popular because many teachers are not trained to implement it. In a situation such as this, it will be very difficult for the teacher to have an acceptable percentage of the effective delivery of the curriculum content, materials and even learning experience to the learner.

Summary and Conclusion

This chapter has examined the various types of curriculum operating in the school. In such analysis, emphasis was focused on the strength and weakness of each of the various types of curriculum with the view of providing and identifying layout for its implementation. The chapter therefore concludes that the teacher's effort is vital in the implementation process of any curriculum as such, the training and retraining of teachers remain vital ingredient for effective implementation of the various, types of curriculum discussed.

CHAPTER THREE

PROCESS OF DEVELOPING A SCHOOL CURRICULUM

Introduction

In the last two chapters, we discussed the concept, types and levels of curriculum that can be identified in the school system. The strength and weakness of each of the various types of curriculum were also stated with the view of providing a guiding framework for the teacher on the effective implementation of each of these types of curriculum. In this chapter therefore, we will examine among others, the various processes of developing a school curriculum. Such processes or stages include: goal determination, planning, tryout, field trial, implementation and quality control mechanism. Each of these stages are discussed relative to the activities involved and the role of evaluation in each stage.

Stages of Developing a School Curriculum

Developing a school curriculum is not an easy task. It takes the combines effort of specialist in different subject areas, working together to fashion out a curriculum. It also requires a lot of time and resources. The period needed to complete the development of a curriculum package varies, depending on the complexity of the programme, level of perfection aimed at by the development team, staffing, technical facilities available, and the intensity of work. But even under the most favourable atmosphere, the time required is usually expressed not in terms of days or weeks or months rather in years. In curriculum centres, all over the world, the time devoted to the development of a programme generally varies from two to five years. In most curriculum projects, one can clearly make a distinction between the various stages in the development process. An attempt is made to distinguish between the various stages. At each stage, the curriculum development team has to focus on a particular task. Accordingly, at each stage, a particular type of evaluation is needed to support the successful development and use of the new programme. The various stages of curriculum development as identified by Akpe (1998), Jeremiah and Alamina (2006) are described below.

Stage 1:
Determination of Goals and Objectives: Goals and objecitves are important variable to be considered in developing a school curriculum. This is because educational programmes do not exist in isolation without due consideration to the society. This implies that the value, trends and other forces that prevail in the society at any given time affect or influence the educational system. The totality of the organizational and educational structures existing in the school and the nature of educational programmes provided through other agencies influence curriculum development. When a

curriculum is designed at the curriculum development centres attention is given to major goals and objectives of the educational system for the given nation. The curriculum centres are only presented with Government decision or policy on education, while the curriculum team's main responsibility is to develop a curriculum that suits the specifications that have been made by the policy makers. For example in Nigeria, the insecurity problems in most parts of Northern Nigeria have paved way for the Almajiri education. In designing the curriculum, National goals of education are considered, goals of education at the basic education level are also considered in line with national aim of education. This is also applicable to the specialised vocational centres established in most parts of the South East and South South geopolitical zones of Nigeria, to take care of girl child or boy child education. In view of this, the role of evaluation becomes restricted at this stage of curriculum development process. However, this does not imply the absence of evaluation. Some assessments are carried out at this stage by team of sociologists, economists, psychologists and anthropologists. Such specialists are consulted to unfold facts about the demographic trends, occupational, economic, and value changes in the society and other vital issues that will be relevant in making decision about the overall aim and objectives of the educational system. Shortly after the determination of goals and objectives, the curriculum development team assume their full responsibilities of evaluating the curriculum. At this stage, the role of evaluation is to point out to policy makers, the need for studying various aspects of social trends in order to make valid decision based on the findings.

Stage 2:
Planning: Planning involves identification of goals, or objectives and fashioning out ways of achieving them. When the goals or objectives have been identified and proper evaluation carried out as stated in the first stage, the next step is to set up a mechanism on how to plan for the success of the curriculum development process. At this stage, issues to be considered may include cost of implementing the curriculum, objective and content area of the curriculum to be developed, methodology, instructional materials, teacher production and utilization. At this stage, objective assessments of each of these variables are carried out with the view of achieving the objectives of the curriculum together with the subject specialist to develop the first version of the resources to be used in the class. This may include writing the text, preparing resource materials and fashioning out students activities plan.

The role of evaluation at this stage becomes manifold. An objective assessment is made about the quality of materials in relation to contemporary trends in the subject area. Such assessment is always carried out by subject specialist. Also at this stage, assessment is made to determine whether the students will be able to learn the materials, master the skills and acquire competences needed for the programme. The focus of assessment is on the cognitive and affective characteristics of the students and the teachers. In a situation were specific learning quipment is needed, it is the duty of the curriculum development team to examine the feasibility and successful use of such materials. At this stage, a preliminary tryout of some of the learning experiences contained in the programme is carried out. The programme is still in the process of preparation, but an aspect of it may be tried out with individuals and small groups of students. The cost of implementing the programme is considered at this stage. In view of this, the following questions may be raised at this stage.

- ❖ Does the programme use the most economical means for obtaining its objectives? Or
- ❖ Is it possible that the school and the students will be able to carry the experiences for implementation?

Honest responses to these questions at this early stage may reduce costly trials and error in the subsequent stages of the programme.

Stage 3:

Tryout and Revision: This stage involves the preliminary testing of learning materials in the programme with a view of finding out the problems involved in the materials and providing adequate solution. Tryout is usually carried out in two to six classes (depending on the population) using samples that represent the sub-group of the population for whom the curriculum has been designed. On this process, selection is carefully done to include only those schools and classes whose teachers participated in the specified teacher training programme and are willing to co-operate with the curriculum development team. At the tryout stage of the curriculum development process, the team carefully observes the teaching/learning process in the classroom situation and utilizes various formative evaluation formats, such as test and pupils worksheet. Both the students and pupils are encouraged to identify and flow in the programme. Data collected from the students and teachers are submitted to various experts for proper assessment. Based on empirical -and expert judgment, decisions are made concerning the specific areas to be modified in the curriculum. After adopting the decisions, the modified version is then prepared by the curriculum development team. At this stage, evaluation becomes very important, in order to avoid interaction that may occur at the field trial stage. The objective of evaluation at the tryout stage is to identify problem areas of the curriculum so that, solution or adjustment can be made before the next stage.

Stage 4:
Field Trial: After a proper assessment of the results from expert and teachers, the curriculum

development team may revise the programme. After the revision of the resource materials and its content, the programme will be subjected to a field trial process using a representative sample of the target population. This stage is characterized by observing the operation of the programme in a situation that one may call the actual implementation. In actual fact, the field trial differs from the tryout stage in the areas of programme characteristics and goal of evaluation. At the tryout stage, the goal of evaluation is to identify areas where there are flows in the programme with the view of providing solution or way forward while at the field trial stage, the goal of evaluation is to examine how the programme will be used in relation to the implementation process. At this stage, the curriculum development team may consider the following fundamental questions

- ❖ Will the programme be suitable to the needs of both urban and rural student population?
- ❖ Are teachers who did not pass through specific training able to teach the new programme?
- ❖ Can the programme be used in schools where the average number of students per class is above thirty?

It is important to note that at the tryout stage, the programme is still available in the provisional form and some aspects of the programme are not yet fully developed. At the tryout stage, there is a closer supervision of the programme by the curriculum development team. In the field trial stage, the team does not maintain a close interaction with the teachers. In this situation, the process of communication becomes more formal. The team at this stage, intervenes, with suggestions on ways of improving the programme where there are difficulties. The field trial stage involves the employment of more realistic and stable form of the programme with limited opportunities to institute programme change.

At this stage, it is important to point out certain issues about evaluation design of the programme. At the tryout stage, two to six classes are usually selected through judgmental sampling but at the field trial stage, most curriculum development centres may utilize about thirty to fifty classes using random sampling technique. The sample size is determined by the size of the system and the cultural, geographical, linguistic and socio-economic factors that pervade the society. The greater the heterogeneity of the school population, the larger the sample needed for the field trial stage. Also, different types of data are collected through such instruments as classroom observation records, formative test and students worksheet. At the field trial stage, following the complexity of the sample, evaluators restrict themselves to collecting only a few types of data. The evaluators at this stage use only multiple choice examination and questionnaire, they rely less on personal observation and impression as in the case at the tryout stage.

Stage 5:
Implementation: After a proper evaluation of the programme at the field trial stage as specified above, the next stage in the curriculum development process is the implementation stage. Curriculum implementation in this situation means the entire process of putting the various decisions made in the field trial stage into practice. Jeremiah (2004) notes that if other stages of the curriculum development process can be executed without active participation or involvement of the school, the implementation stage is largely within the province of the school to accomplish. Mkpa (1978) explaines that curriculum implementation is the classroom effort of staff and student in putting into operation what is obtained in the curriculum document. Mkpa further states that it involves the task of transplanting the curriculum document into operating curriculum by the combined effort of students, teachers and others concerned. It also means an open use of the programme in the entire school system. In some countries with centralized educational systems, a programme may either become compulsory for all schools of a certain type, or may be among a list of authorized alternative programmes for which each school chooses the most suitable for its needs. Whichever be the case, implementation will involve certain changes within the school system. At first, teacher training's to be adjusted and modified to

53

meet the standard requirement of the new programme. New teaching methods, strategies, learning styles or class management practices may be the focus of adjustment or modification in the teacher training programme. At this stage, teachers should be trained and re-trained to monitor the programme because they hold the key to the success or failure of the programme. The third issue to examine, is on making appropriate changes in the National Examination system, if it exists. As the programme is changed, there is the need for national examinations to be reviewed in line with the requirements of the new programme. At this stage, the goal of evaluation is to examine the efficiency of the changes and adjustments made mostly at the preceding stages. This may be carried out through the observation of the teachers, experts and other stakeholders.

Stage 6:
Quality Control: After implementing a curriculum for some period the curriculum may deteriorate over time. This may involve deterioration in part or whole, and by implication the entire curriculum may deteriorate or part of it. Part of it implies the curriculum objective, content, methodology, instructional materials, teacher production and utilization and even the evaluation procedure. When this occurs, an effective quality control mechanism should be instituted. Hence, quality control involves all the mechanism instituted to ensure that a school curriculum stands the test of time. Elements of such

quality control mechanism may include seminars, workshops, conferences, pre-service and in-service training programmes, programme evaluations etc, organized by various professional bodies, agencies and parastatals. Proper quality control mechanism may reveal whether some or all aspects of the programme should be altered or replaced. To this view, quality control may be geared towards the updating of an existing programme or the development of a new one. This supports the view of Wheeler as noted by Jeremiah and Alamina (2006) that curriculum development process should be seen as a cyclic activity. Several curriculum centres that developed innovative programme several years ago are now contemplating producing second generation programme, which respond better to the existing needs of the system than the previous ones. The quality control result may serve as an indicator that calls for attention to the need, where necessary, for innovative activities.

The focal point of evaluation at this stage is on the success of the entire programme, which include competency. The focus of evaluation may be on a particular chapter of the programme, particular activity associated with its use, such as organization of the curriculum content or a particular type of instructional materials included in the textbook, such as a teacher's guide, audio-visual aids, enrichment supplement, experimental materials or teacher training programme. Also, evaluation may be carried out only in one specific aspect of the component. For example, it may focus on such aspects as quality of textbooks, illustration, clarity of explanation, the readability of the text, the sequence of learning experience or adequacy of the exercise. Such unique aspects of the programme as a whole may also be investigated.

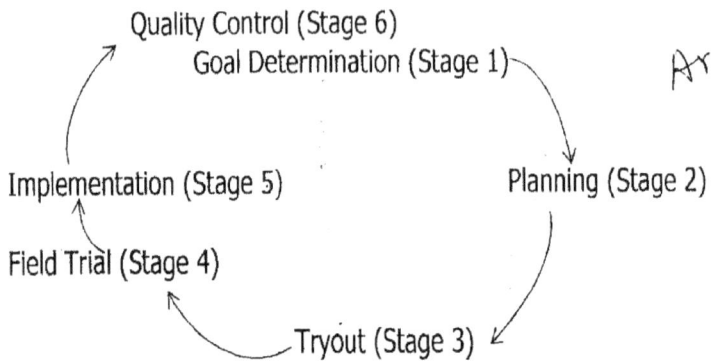

Quality Control (Stage 6)
Goal Determination (Stage 1)
Implementation (Stage 5)
Planning (Stage 2)
Field Trial (Stage 4)
Tryout (Stage 3)

Figure 2:   Stages of Curriculum Development Process

Curriculum Development Agencies
Curriculum development agencies are somehow difficult to select or pinpoint. In any case, an agent is supposed to be one who causes an educational innovation to take place or one who originates such an innovation. Nwafor (2007) as cited by Oteh and Akuma (2010) states that curriculum agents or agencies are any body, group or unit that systematically contributes, solves, or attempt to solve new or existing problems in education. Hence, curriculum development agencies can be described as individuals or organization whose interest can

56

contribute to the development of a school curriculum. Such interest can influence development of parts or total restructuring of the entire school programme. Some of the agents and agencies of curriculum development are explained below.

The Teacher:
The teacher's role is very crucial in curriculum development process. Hence, the National Policy on Education (2004) stated that no system of education can rise above the quality of its teachers. This simply implies that teachers hold the key to the success or failure of the entire system of education. In the first part of this chapter, we explained the various steps or stages of curriculum development process and pointed out that if any other stage can be executed without active participation or involvement of the school, the implementation stage is largely within the province of the school. In the school, the teacher serves as a link between the learners and the - external community. The teacher gathers useful data as they interact with learners in the classroom. Such data are vital elements for curriculum development. By adopting new relevant teaching methods, and strategies, they introduce innovation with educational system. Such innovation comes as a result of comparative analysis of the best approach that can enhance achievement, retention and even the development of positive attitude towards learning. The teacher as a- member of a given community is quite closer to the members

of the community. He gathers constructive criticisms from the community about the school and provides useful advice to the school authorities. Such as the P.T.A, School Supervisors, Head Teachers, etc. Such advice can also be presented in workshops, seminars and conferences if given the opportunity to do so. Such issues provide a good stepping stone or platform for curriculum development.

Ministries of Education:
Curriculum development in Nigeria is the statutory role of the Federal Ministry of Education with its branches in all the states of the Federation. Each state also has the State Ministry of Education, vested with the responsibility of formulating policies as regards to the educational sector. Apart from establishing, maintaining, equipping and staffing of schools, it also formulates policies that govern the school and indeed the educational sector. Apart from implementing the agreed policies, the ministries of education some time organize seminars, workshops and conferences. The communique from such fora organization provide a good tool for curriculum development.

Government Agencies:
 These are various governmental bodies that have been involved in curriculum development in Nigeria. Such agencies include the Nigerian Educational Research and Development Council (NERDC), Comparative Education Study and Adaptation Centre (CESAC), National Universities Commission

(NUC), National Board for Technical Education (NBTE) and International Centre for Educational Evaluation (ICEE). Some of these agencies relative to their role in curriculum development are discussed below.

Nigerian Educational Research and Development Council (NERDC):

This agency was formally known as the Nigerian Educational Research Council (NERC) established shortly after independence. It was initially an arm of the Federal Ministry of Education. It became an autonomous body through decree No. 31 of August 31st, 1972. The body was vested with the mandate of facilitating the implementations of the recommendations of the 1969 curriculum conference. In 1988 the body was merged with three other agencies namely: The Comparative Education Study and Adaptation Centre (CESAC); the Nigerian Book Development Council (NBD); and the Nigerian Language Centre (NLC) to form the Nigerian Educational Research and Development Council (NERDC) through Act No. 53 of 1988.

The NERDC was established as a result of the demand by Nigerians for a system of education that would recognize their needs and aspirations. Before this time, the Nigerian Education was faulted for its lack of relevance. The NERC initiated the National Curriculum Conference held in Lagos in September 1969. The aim, goal and objectives of Nigerian Education were fully articulated as it involves all levels of education. Shortly after the conference various workshop and seminars were also held to properly interpret the recommendations of the conference. This culminated in the publication of the National Policy on Education first published in 1977, revised in 1981, 1998 and 2004 respectively. This implies that the present system of education in Nigeria is the brain child of the 1969 curriculum conference.

The mission statement of the NERDC is: creating the enabling environment in which educational research and development activities will thrive; and in the process, it will not only encourage collaboration with international development partners but with also foster public private partnership in a bid to render educational research and development efforts sustainable and need-driven.

Some major functions of the Council include the following:

- ❖ To formulate and implement national policy on book development.
- ❖ To encourage and promote reading culture through a continuous research into the needs of Nigerian readers.
- ❖ To undertake and promote book development and local authorship.
- ❖ To promote the development of curricula of all levels of the educational system.
- ❖ To produce syllabuses and instructional materials for various languages taught in the Nigerian school system.

❖ To identify, encourage, promote and coordinate, research into educational problems in Nigeria.
❖ To promote and develop Nigerian languages.
❖ To coordinate language development projects throughout Nigeria, and prepare an overall design for language research needs.
❖ To maintain relationship with corresponding educational research and development bodies in Nigeria and other parts of the world.
❖ To sponsor national and international conferences as may be relevant to the functions of the Council.
❖ To carry out any other activities likely to assist in the performance of the functions imposed on the council by the Act.

Comparative Education Study and Adaptation Centre (CESAC):

This agency was founded in 1968 at the University of Lagos with a grant from Ford Foundation. The establishment of CESAC was part of the centralized National effort to evolve more suitable educational system that is adopted to suit the mental aptitude, occupation and traditional system of Nigerian. The cardinal role of CESAC was to appraise and identify defective areas in the Nigerian Educational system and to proffer solution. It went on to compare past experienced and current educational practices within and outside the shores of Nigeria. Over the years, it helped to identify problems facing secondary schools and proffered solution. It has also introduced innovations at the secondary school level in science and other subject areas. In the various secondary school subjects, CESAC has made a remarkable curriculum improvement. Well written textsbooks were produced in science and other subjects under the umbrella of the Nigerian Secondary School Science Project (NSSSP) CESAC also contributed significantly towards the development of social studies curriculum in Nigeria. The body has been merged with three other agencies into the present Nigeria Education Research and Development Council (NERDC).

National Universities Commission (NUC):
This body is charged with the responsibility of establishing the minimum standard in all universities in Nigeria. The functions of NUC are as follows:

❖ Accreditation of existing programmes in the universities.

❖ Controlling or regulating the introduction of new courses.

❖ Advising the Federal Government on all academic matters in the universities.

❖ Stipulating the range of courses to be offered indicating the core courses and elective ones for all students and authorities concerned.

❖ Inspection of the physical structure and facilities available in universities to ascertain their appropriateness in enhancing teaching and learning in universities.

❖ Constant monitoring of all universities programmes, with a view of replacing obsolete ones with new ones.

NUC is vested with the power to close down any university that does not meet the stipulated standard, relative to programme and infrastructural development. It can award "interim or full" accreditation in respect of university programme after each exercise. It also has power to refuse further admission into any programme that does not scale through an accreditation exercise.

National Board for Technical Education (NBTE)
This curriculum development body was established through Decree No. 9
of 11th January 1977 with its functions as follows:

❖ To advise and coordinate all matters regarding technical and vocational education in Nigeria.

❖ To make recommendations on the National policy for the full development of technical and vocational education for the training of technicians, craftsmen and other middle-level manpower needs of the country in the industrial, commercial and other relevant fields.

❖ To advise on the maximization of the use of available facilities in colleges of technology and polytechnics to avoid unnecessary duplication and waste but also ensuring their adequacy to. the manpower needs of the country.

❖ To recommend the location for the establishment of new polytechnics and colleges of technology where and when necessary.

❖ To advise the Federal Government on proper funding of polytechnics and colleges of technology and other technical institutions.

❖ To act as an agency for channeling all external aids to polytechnics and colleges of technology in Nigeria.

❖ To advise on and harmonize entry requirements and duration of courses at technical institutions.

❖ To lay down standard skills to be attained and to continually review such standards as necessitated by technological and national needs.

❖ To review methods of assessment of students and trainees.

❖ To develop a scheme of National Certification for technicians and other skilled personnels in collaboration with ministries and organizations having technical training programmes.

❖ To undertake periodic review of the terms and conditions of personnels in polytechnics and colleges of technology and make recommendations for the Federal Government.

National Commission for Colleges of Education (NCCE):

This body was established on 13th January, 1989. It is among the agencies that control standards in Nigerian institution of higher learning. The functions of NCCE include:

❖ To advice and coordinate all aspects of teacher education outside the universities and polytechnics.

❖ To make recommendations on the National Policy necessary for full development of teacher education and the training of teachers.

❖ Accreditation of certificate and all academic programmes of colleges of education.

❖ To advice on and be able to harmonize entry requirement and duration of courses at the Colleges of Education, to review methods of assessment of students in collaboration with the Ministry of Education and the university to which the colleges are affiliated.

❖ To lay down minimum standards for all programmes of teacher education. Minimum entry requirement, minimum credit load to be carried by each student per semester, minimum number of teachers per department and general student/teacher ratio.

It is important to note that before the establishment of NCCE, colleges of education in Nigeria maintained different standards, in terms of management, funding and production of curricular materials. Such standards were provided by their affiliating universities in line with guidelines provided by their State Ministries of Education. The need for maintenance of a uniform or centralized curriculum model by all NCE awarding institutions in Nigeria led to the establishment of the NCCE in November, 1990. It became fully operational during the 1991/1992 academic session. In realization of the fact that curriculum development is a continual process, the NCCE has established subject panels among teachers in various subject areas in the colleges of education. The panels monitor and ensure the implementation of the minimum standards provided by the commission. The commission constantly utilize the data provided by the panel for programme review, and innovation relative to workshop, in-service programme, conferences, etc, all aimed at improving the standards of teacher education.

The West African Examination Council (WAEC):
The West Africa Examination Councils (WAEC) is the first indigenous examination body in Nigeria and most countries within the West African sub-region. The body was founded in the year 1953 and was vested with the power of harmonizing examinations in West Africa mostly within the Anglophone countries of Gambia, Ghana, Nigeria and Sierra Leone. Its headquarters is located at Accra, Ghana. In Nigeria, zonal offices are located at Benin City,

Enugu, Ibadan, Ikeja, Jos, Kaduna, Sokoto, Maiduguri and Owerri. Other branches are at Abeokuta, Garki, (Abuja), Akure, Bauchi, Calabar, Ilorin, Kano, Katsina, Makudi, Mina, Port-Harcourt, Umuahia, Uyo and Yola.

As an internationally recognized body, it dictates the tempo or the direction of curriculum innovation and change by regulating and standardizing secondary education programme in those countries. Some of the functions of WAEC include:

- ❖ Establishing secondary school syllabus and ensuring its periodic revision.
- ❖ Monitoring the implementation of the syllabus in secondary schools, inspecting physical structures such as science laboratories, technology workshops, examination halls to ensure the school readiness for science experiment and practicals.
- ❖ Organizing workshops, conferences and seminars for resource persons, teachers and WAEC staff.
- ❖ Selling and conducting the senior school certificate examination in line with prescribed standards.
- ❖ Establishing effective marking exercises at both zonal and branch levels for SSCE examination papers using standard marking schemes in all subjects.

❖ Conducting external examinations (WASCE & GCE) for candidates who are not in secondary schools. This is to enable them obtain the knowledge and certificate for self-employment and admission into tertiary levels of education.

❖ Awarding certificates to candidates who took the WASCE, SSCE examinations. Such certificate provides recipients with minimum requirements and qualifications for admission into institutions of higher learning; and workforce.

National Examination Council (NECO):

This examination body was established in 1999. By its mandate, it took over the responsibilities of the National Board for Educational Measurement (NBEM) which was created in 1992. NECO offices have been created in all states of the Federation including the Federal Capital Territory (FCT). In addition, NECO zonal offices are located at Bauchi, Ibadan, Markudi, Owerri, Ilorin, Ore, Asaba, Damaturu, Enugu, Lagos, Port-Harcourt, Sokoto, Uyo, Yola and Kano. Its administration is organized into six departments headed by Directors and the office of the Registrar.

The Council is vested with the responsibilities of conducting the Senior Secondary School Certificate

Examination (SSCE) for both internal and external candidates. According to Oteh and Akuma (2010), the first SSCE external examination was held from November 9 to December 3, 2002. The examination took place in 846 centers in Nigeria with a population of 224,788 (127,983 male and 96,806 female). NECO also conducts junior secondary schools certificate examinations for candidates in third year of junior secondary schools. The categories of schools involved are Unity schools, Armed forces schools and others controlled by the Federal Government. NECO also conduct common entrance examination for pupils into Federal Unity Schools all over Nigeria.

National Business and Technical Examination Board (NABTEB):
The National Business and Technical Examination Board (NABTEB) was established through Decree No. 70 of August 1993 with its headquarters at Benin City, Edo State Nigeria. This body was created to take over the functions of the exams that were conducted by the Royal Society of Arts (RSA) of London, City and Guilds (C&G) of London and the West African Examination Council (WAEC) in keeping with the provisions of the National Policy on Education. The board's mission statement is geared towards conducting Technical and Business Examinations, issue results/ certificates with a view of meeting the needs of candidates who wish to use them for both academic programmes and employment.

Functions of the Board include:

- ❖ Conducting common entrance examinations into technical colleges and allied institutions.
- ❖ Issuing results, certificates and make awards in examinations conducted by the Board.
- ❖ Conducting other special examinations on behalf of or in collaboration with other examination bodies or agencies such as London Chamber of Commerce and Institute of Chartered Accountants of Nigeria, etc.
- ❖ Monitoring colleging and keeping records of Continuous Assessment in Technical Colleges and Allied Institutions towards the award of certificate in National Business and Technical Examinations.
- ❖ Taking over the conduct of Technical and Business Examination formally conducted by the Royal Society of Arts of London, City and Guilds of London and West African Examination Council.
- ❖ Conducting examinations leading to the award of the NationalTechnical Certificate (NTC); Advance Technical Certificate (ATC); National Business Certificate (NBC); Advance National Business Certificate (ANBC).
- ❖ Conducting research, publishing statistics and other information in order to develop

appropriate examination, tests, and syllabus in technical business studies.

❖ Preparing an annual report on standards of examinations and other related issues.

The National Teachers' Institute (NTI):

The National Teacher Institute (NTI) was established in 1976 through Decree 7 of 1978 promulgated two years after its inception. The institute was originally set up to manage the Teacher Grade II (TC II) examination in the three core subjects (Mathematics, English Language, and General Paper). These are the three core subjects which were federally examined for the award of the TC II, which was almost the highest qualification needed for teaching in the primary schools. Following the 1977 National Policy recommendation of NCE as the minimum qualification for teaching in Nigeria and the closure of Teachers' Training Colleges, the responsibilities of NTI were widened to include evaluating and awarding of TC II Certificate to teachers who failed in their first or second attempt. Also, in response to the National Policy directives, the role of NTI was further widened to include mounting courses leading to the award of the NCE in certain subject areas. According to Sele (2011) the National Teachers Institute was established specifically to:

❖ Train and upgrade all qualified Grade II teachers to the NCE level.

❖ Provide basic background for those of them who would later wish to pursue their discipline.

❖ Help produce the needed teachers for the successful implementation of the National Policy on education.

At present the institute runs NCE programme in subject areas such as Christian Religious Knowledge (CRK), Cultural and Creative Arts (CCA), English Language (Eng.L, Integrated Science (ITS), Islamic Religious Studies (IRS), Mathematics (Maths); others include Social Studies (SOS), Primary Education Studies (PES) and finally Education (EDU). NTI also runs Academic Diploma Programme in some special areas such as Early Childhood, School Management, etc and Post Graduate Diploma in Education (PGDE). These programmes are run through the Distant Learning System (DLS).

Subject Associations:
In Nigeria, we have many subject associations that promote curriculum development in specific disciplines and education at large. Prominent among these subject associations include Science Teachers Association of Nigeria (STAN), Mathematics Association of Nigeria (MAN), Social Studies Association of Nigeria (SOSAN). Others include Curriculum Organization of Nigeria (CON), Counselling Association of Nigeria (CASSON), etc. In this paper, we will discuss the activities of Science

Teachers Association of Nigeria (STAN) and Curriculum Organization of Nigeria (CON).

Science Teachers of Nigeria (STAN):
This curriculum development body came into existence in Nigeria in 1957 with the aim of promoting science teaching at the primary, secondary and teachers training colleges. Later it co-opted science teachers at the tertiary levels. STAN is a strong professional organization whose major aim is as follows:

- ❖ The promote of co-operation among members and the improvement of the standard of science education in the country.
- ❖ To provide a forum for science teachers on matters of common interest.
- ❖ To help science teachers keep in touch with developments in science and its application in industry and commerce.
- ❖ To popularize the teaching of science in the country.
- ❖ To perform such other functions incidental or necessary for the realization of these objectives.

Activities of STAN in Nigeria
STAN has actually promoted science teaching in Nigeria by undertaking in these activities:

- ❖ Organization of periodic conferences. The conferences also include workshops, seminars, lectures, subject panel meeting science faire, quiz, exhibition of instructional materials and teaching aids, books, experiments and field trip to places of scientific interest.
- ❖ Organization of seminars and workshop in Chemistry, Biology, Physics, Agricultural Science, Integrated Science, Mathematics, Primary Science and Teacher Education.
- ❖ Preparation of science teachers in collaboration with such bodies as WAEC, JAMB, NERDC, NECO, Ministries of Education and other related agencies in the production of science curriculum resources.
- ❖ Collaboration with international bodies with similar interest through participation in international conferences.
- ❖ Through these activities, STAN has been able to create and coordinate eight subject panels for promoting teaching and learning effectiveness in the subject areas. The subjects are: Primary Science, Agricultural Science, Biology, Chemistry, Physics, Mathematics, Integrated Science, and Teacher Education. The publications of STAN include:

- ❖ Journal of Science Teachers Association of Nigeria.
- ❖ Proceedings of Annual Conferences and National Workshops since 1982 till date.
- ❖ STAN Bulletin to keep members up to date on its activities.
- ❖ Nigerian Integrated Science Programme (NISP) which include pupils text 1 — 3 for JSS students including teachers guide.
- ❖ Biology, Physics, Chemistry and Agriculture texts for senior secondary school students, and
- ❖ STAN Science Teachers' Handbook.

Curriculum Organization of Nigeria (CON)
This is an association of curriculum experts, teachers, administrators and scholars who are interested in curriculum research and development. The organization was formally established in 1982 with the following objectives.

- ❖ To bring together all persons interested in curriculum development for the purpose of sharing knowledge in the problem and practice of curriculum.
- ❖ To promote training in curriculum research, development and evaluation, and
- ❖ To encourage the publication and dissemination of appropriate types of formation in curriculum development,

research and evaluation for all levels of education.

Since its inception, Mkpa and Izuagba (2012) note that the organization has been involved in the following activities.

❖ Organizing annual conferences, workshops, seminars and regular meeting of persons interested in curriculum research and development.

❖ Disseminating information through bulletins, newsletters and journal articles.

❖ Setting up task forces to carry out specific projects curriculum development and research.

❖ Making recommendations to schools and ministries of education concerning school curriculum and other aspects that may affect the school curriculum at large.

Summary and Conclusion

In this chapter, we have explained the various stages of curriculum development process and also the agencies involved in curriculum development process. Such agencies work with various stakeholders in the task of developing a school curriculum. The chapter therefore concludes that curriculum development process is not an easy task. It takes the combined effort of specialists in different subject areas working together to fashion out a curriculum.

CHAPTER FOUR

CURRICULUM INNOVATION AND CHANGE

Introduction

In the previous chapter, we discussed curriculum development process and identified the role of quality control mechanism as it provides information that may call for curriculum innovation. Thus in this chapter, we will examine the concept of curriculum innovation and change, strategies for curriculum innovation and change, factors for curriculum change and innovation, theories and strategies for curriculum innovation and change.

What is Curriculum Innovation and Change?

The concept of curriculum innovation and change are often used interchangeably as if they mean the same thing but in actual fact, they mean different things. Unruh and Alexander (1974) see innovation as the introduction of a novel factor perceived as new by a given school or community, supported by a driving force, and implemented as a practical advance that deviates from established or traditional forms. Another scholar Miles (1973) defines innovation as a deliberate novel, specific change which is thought to be more affective in accomplishing the goals of a system. The implication of the above definition is that innovation is often willed and planned for. It does not occur spontaneously or haphazardly. So if there is a deliberate novel and specific change in the curriculum on the basis of the fact that it will be more effective in the attainment of the objectives, we conclude that an innovation has taken place. Such innovation can be in terms of goals or objectives of the programme, content, curriculum materials, teacher production and utilization. Change according to Miles (1973), refers to those noticeable differences or deviations occurring between first and second periods. That is to say, there has been a noticeable modification in the structure of the school system in-terms of its processes, goals and objectives between a given time.

Jeremiah and Alamina (2006) explain that curriculum Innovation means changing certain aspects of the school without changes in fundamental conception or original structure. It also means the differences introduced into our school system that are capable of affecting the curriculum in one way or another. On the other hand, they further explain that curriculum change involves the transformation of the entire curriculum scheme including its design, goals, content, learning activities and scopes. It also involves change in the value assumption on which all the mentioned areas of the curriculum are based.

Curriculum innovation is based on, the responses to change in the needs of the society, development of new understanding concerning the teaching/learning process and assessment of the effectiveness of the programme. For example, social studies programme are created in responds to the needs of the society and as these needs change so too will social studies instruction change or risk becoming an outmoded part of the curriculum. The condition under which these needs change will vary widely. In some cases a dramatic shift in the programme will be required, while in others, it may be necessary only to modify certain aspects.

Aspect of Educational Innovations in Nigeria
The society is dynamic and as such, all the institutions that operate in such a given society should take such a dynamic model. Education as we will consider here is a dynamic instrument of change, for this reason educational policies and programmes are constantly reviewed to ensure adequacy and adaptation to national aims and objective. In Nigeria, so many educational innovations have taken place, which have altered the educational system in different ways. The first seed of Western education in Nigeria was sowed in 1842, which marked the arrival of the Christian Missionaries. For the first time, Nigeria witnessed an organized system of education. This was a departure from the traditional system of education, which was in existence before the coming of the white man. In this new system, people were taught how to read, write and solve arithmetic problems (3Rs), the objectives of education was to produce clerks,

interpreters and catechists, mainly for the rapid spread of Christianity in the various parts of Nigeria. In 1882, the colonial government began to intervene in the affairs of education, by 1922, the Phelp-Stokes report titled "Education in Africa" was produced and this paved way to the 1925 memorandum of education. In this era, education was gradually transformed to suit local needs. Hussey, the Director of Education in 1930 reviewed the entire educational system and made some proposals for changes. He recommended a six-year primary education instead of the existing eight years. He also proposed for a vocational higher education, which led to the establishment of the Yaba Higher College in 1932. The Eliot Commission report of 1943 led to the establishment of the University College Ibadan in 1948. Thus, so many educational innovations that were introduced in our educational system came into reality as a result of the series of ordinance, memoranda, and reports of commissions.

Other educational innovation in Nigeria started in the 1950s to 1960. This era is referred, to by many scholars as age of self-determination. The introduction of the U.P.E. into the Western Region in January 1955 under the leadership of Pa Obafemi Awolowo. The proposal for the U.P.E. was made in 1952 by the Western Region Minister of Education Chief S.O. Awokoya. Between 1952 and 1954, considerable efforts were made to meet the 1955 target. A period of years was used in planning for its implementation. The West embarked on a massive teacher training programme, supervision of secondary school, and introduction of technical education and secondary modern school and many schools were built. In January 1 7th 1955, the scheme was launched.

The introduction of the U.P.E. scheme in the West was a big challenge to the other regions, the North, East and the Colony Lagos. The East followed suit and on February 1957, the U.P.E scheme was launched. Since no adequate planning was made, nearly all the new schools were faced with the problem of untrained teachers and lack of infrastructural facilities. The scheme ran into difficulties right from the beginning and by 1958, most teachers were laid off. This motivated the missionaries mostly the Roman Catholic mission to take over their schools. The scheme was introduced in January 1957. In the North, the scheme was properly delayed as a result of funding problems, large population of school children and political and religious problems, which resisted the spread of Western education by the Moslems. After the attainment of independence in 1960, Nigeria began to control the affairs of education without the difference of our colonial masters. The first outcry after independent was that education should be marched with the needs child, and that the curriculum in the schools at all levels should be relevant to the needs and aspiration of the Nigeria child. The Ashby report on higher education of 1960 to the 1969 curriculum conference contributed greatly in transforming our educational system from the colonial flavour to a more realistic education, tailored to meet the people needs and aspiration.

Another major change that occurs in our education system during the post independent era was government takeover of schools in 1973. At this time, primary and secondary schools were taken over from the mission and private enterprises. This implies a uniform system of education at all levels and uniform conditions of service for teachers and other non-academic staff. In this era, education was seen as a means of national re-orientation, reconstruction and reconciliation. Education was to be made available to all irrespective of age gender, cultural group and religion. The government takeover of schools shortly after the war was as a result of the clamour for complete government control of the educational system.

Shortly after the government takeover of schools in 1973, the Federal Military Government launched a universal primary education scheme on 6th September 1976. Education was made free and compulsory mostly at the primary school level. Tuition fee was eradicated in all primary institutions of learning. By 1979 the second U.P.E. project failed as a result of inadequate planning, poor statistics, poor funding and corruption. It should be crystal clear in our mind that the first major mistake of the U.P.E. was the idea of the Federal Government shouldering the responsibility of the scheme. No country in the world can boast of a complete free education. Education should be ajoint venture between the Federal Government, State Government, Local Government and the parents.

The greatest change that have reshaped our educational system in Nigeria is the implementation of the new National Policy on Education called 6—3 —3 —4 system. The New National Policy was the brainchild of the 1969 curriculum conference and the 1973 National Seminar on education. The 6 —3 —3 —4 system was a great departure from the 6— 5—2—3/4 system that was inherited from our colonial masters.

Some Primary School Curriculum Innovations In Nigeria

Adewole (1999) reports that a lot of external influences and foreign curricular motivated many of the curriculum innovations in science at the primary school level, some of the foreign curricular included the following. Elementary Study of Science (ESS) of 1960, Science a Process Approach (SAPA) of 1962; Science Education Project of 1970. As a result of those influences many primary science curriculum projects were put into place in Nigeria. Some of those primary science projects are identified by Mkpa(1987) Adewole (1999) and Jeremiah (2004).

The African Primary Science Project (A.P.S.P):
This was one of the earliest curriculum innovation projects in science at the primary school level. It was launched in Kano in January 1965 by the Ford foundation of Africa and Educational Development Centre Massachusetts. The programme was later changed to Science Education Project for Africa (SEPA). This project take into consideration the interest of the African child in learning science by utilizing African environment. With this approach the child was able to develop the habit of looking at his environment in a way that would elicit questions while and to such questions could be found through experimentation. The cardinal objectives of this project was to bring with the reach of every child the benefit of relevant and excellence education, by utilizing the accumulated knowledge and technique of science as a vehicle to furnish him with the requisite skills, which will enable him to make rational judgment about his total environment.

Adewole (1999) states that SEPA produced many materials mostly inform of teachers guide or handbook. This is because SEPA saw the teacher's role as crucial in the preparation of learning materials and diagnosing peoples needs and difficulties. SEPA therefore devote sufficient time and energy in training and retraining of teachers because the teachers have to diagnose and appraise the pupils efforts, their imagination, excitement and frustration.

The Bendel Primary Science Project (BPSP):

The Bendel Primary Science Project was initiated in Benin City in 1966 with financial and technical assistance from UNESCO, UNICEF and UNDP, the development was drawn from the State Ministry of Education. Various institutions of higher learning in Bendel State and UNESCO experts produced in 1972 a series of pupil's textbook known as "Science is discovering" together with teachers guide. The project, which was coordinated at the science curriculum development centre, Abraka, emphasized the use of discovery method, and focused on the Childs environment and the acceleration of the development of desirable (Scientific) attitude, interest and certain basic concept. The produced materials were latter trial tested, revised and introduced into primary schools all over Bendel State.

Science Programme of the Primary Education Improvement Project (SPEIP):

Mkpa (1987) reports that this primary education improvement project was initiated in 1970 at institute of education. Alimadu Bello, University Zaria. The project was developed with financial and technical assistance from UNESCO, UNICEF, USAID and the British Council. The curriculum materials produced from the project were series)f pupil's textbooks (bks.1-6) and teachers guide, which provides detailed information for the teachers to carry out science activities, which must have been specified in the pupils text. The project aimed at

85

making children think and study science like scientist thus it adopted the philosophy of the American Association for the Advancement of Science (AAAS) process and skills for achieving this aim will emphasis on the following processes of science such observation, measuring, classification, using number manipulating, communicating, predicting, information, interpreting, formulating hypothesis and experimenting.

"Sayensi" Ife Six Years Yoruba Primary Science Project:

This was part of an enlarged Ife six years Yoruba primary education project initiated in 1970 at the University of Ife under the chairmanship of Professor Babatunde Fafunwa, the then Director of the institute of education university of Ife. The project takes into consideration to uses of mother tongue in the teaching and learning of to following primary school subjects such as English Mathematics, Yoruba, Cultural and Creative Arts, Social Studies, Family Living and Physical Education.

The main component of the project we comprehensive syllabus for each subject, scheme of work, pupils texts, pupils work book, teachers guide, language medium serving text, visual aids and examination data ban The "Sayensi" writing group of the curriculum development team did a lot of work as the group has to battle with writing science concept in Yoruba as non of the group member learnt or taught science in Yoruba before.

The group therefore has to set up a lexical committee especially to select the right choice of words and concept that would correct express in Yoruba for those science concepts and expressions not easily identifiable with Yoruba language. The purpose was to borrow the foreign words using Yoruba orthography.

It is pertinent to note that the use of mother tongue (Yoruba) in the teaching of science was indeed a unique pioneering effort, which unfortunately has neither been further adopted for use in all Yoruba schools and beyond nor has there been further research effort over the years to vigorously explore the teaching of science in mother tongue. Today, virtually all primary schools in Nigeria still teach science in English Language to pupils thereby creating to them a concentric circle of difficulties in understanding science, which they later carry on to secondary schools.

National Primary School Science Project (N.P.S.S.P):
The idea of having a core-curriculum for primary science led to the National Primary Science Project (N.P.S.S.P) later called National Primary Science and Mathematics Project (N.P.S.M.P). This project was initiated in 1978 under the direct supervision of the Federal Ministry of Education and coordinated by the Nigerian Education Research Council (NERC). A primary school science curriculum panel was earlier set up under the chairmanship of Dr. B.C.E. Nwosu,

the chief education officer in the Federal Ministry of Education with representatives from NERC, Universities of Ife, Abu, Lagos, Nsukka and representatives from the following states; Ondo, Lagos, Sokoto, Imo, Benue and Bauchi States.

The panel was given some terms of reference as observed by Jeremiah (2004) and set up to work immediately by reviewing the various objectives of the primary science Programme operating in different states of the Federation with a view of identifying the common or core elements on them and therefore checking whether such elements is consistent with the objectives of primary science education as stipulated in the National Policy on Education. After many deliberation, the panel recommended that science education at the primary school level should enable the child to:

- Observe and explore the environment
- Develop basic science process skills
- Develop functional knowledge of science concepts principles
- Develop a scientific attitude; such as curiosity, critical reflection and objectivity.
- To apply the skills and knowledge gained through science to solving every day problem in environment.
- Develop confidence and self-reliance through problem solving activities in science.

- Develop functional awareness and sensitivity to orderliness and beauty in nature.

In summary the panel produced a core curriculum syllabus for primary science with instructional units organized into six columns of topic, performance objective, content, activities, materials and evaluation. Adewole (1999) reports that this is the first time in the history of science teaching in Nigeria that emphasis was laid in these six areas. Jeremiah (2004) proves details of the core-content system which is currently in use with modification in primary schools of Nigeria.

Some Secondary School Curriculum Innovation in Nigeria

At this stage, we will examine two major curriculum innovations or curriculum projects. Such projects include the Nigerian Integrated Science Project and the Nigerian Secondary School Project.The Nigerian Integrated Science Project: One of the major setbacks of the colonial education is its lack of relevance to the need and aspiration of the Nigerian child. It also de-emphasized the study of science and technology. This led to the 1969 curriculum conference, which automatically calumniated to the adoption of a new National Policy on Education. Shortly after, Nigerian began to identify the importance of science as a vital tool to a better technological breakthrough. The need to re-examine both what to teach in and how to teach it led to both institution and professional bodies to identify themselves with National effort towards curriculum reforms in science education. In responding to this, the Science Teachers Association of Nigeria (STAN), set up curriculum Development Committee in the Science subjects such as Biology, Chemistry and Physics. In 1969, the association published its first newsletter vol. 1 on the Nigerian Integrated Science Project for students in class one and class two of the Nigerian secondary school. The newsletter contained guidelines for affecting a course on integrated science at the junior forms of the secondary schools. At present, STAN now offers to secondary schools set of materials such as textbooks, teachers guide, instructional materials etc. such materials are the product of outcome of conference, seminars, workshops and research works.

Requirements for Curriculum Innovation and Change:

Changing a curriculum means in a way changing an institution which involves changing individuals. To change individuals involves two types of changes, which include; the cognitive aspect. This has to do with changes in the way individuals are oriented to the world around them relative to what is perceived and appreciated. Emotional orientation involves what the individual feels to be important, what he is motivated to do and what emotional investment or satisfaction he makes in his goal. The change is effective to the extent that the two became integrated.

An effective strategy for curriculum change and innovation therefore must proceed on a double agenda, working simultaneously to change ideas about the curriculum and to change human dynamics. In order to achieve both, the strategy of curriculum innovation and change therefore must proceed on double agenda working simultaneously to change ideas about the curriculum and to change human dynamics. In order to achieve both, the strategy of curriculum innovation and change requires a methodology which may be summarized as follows.

Curriculum Innovation and Change Require a Systematic Sequence of work which Deals with all Aspect of the Curriculum:
A piece meal approach, no matter how effective does not produce efficient change i.e. either in thinking about a curriculum or in the actual practice. Thus, plan strategy must be established, a sequence of steps that will effect curriculum change. In initiating curriculum change, were does one begin? What is the order of steps or what must be followed by a given group etc.

Curriculum Innovation and Change involve creating a Condition for Productive Work:
 Under what condition does productivity flourish or languish? What process needs to be employed to enhance creative productivity? Which human relative operates, and how does one deal with these what roles does much device as committees, study

91

groups, individul experimentation and work team play and how do these operate in the various sequential order?

Effecting Curriculum Innovation or Change involves a large amount of Training:
New skills need to be learned, new cognitive perspectives must be acquired, new mode of thinking need to be initiated. Most curriculum decisions no matter their scope require application of theoretical principles. What balance of theoretical - insight and practical know-how is needed? The questions to be raised are; that kind of training does one require, and how and when should it be provided.

Innovation and Change always involves Human and Emotional Factor:
In effort to change thinking about the curriculum, one also need to change people attitudes towards what is significant about role, purpose and motivation. To effect change mean to destroy dependencies on previous habit and technique of work. With whatever personal meaning these have, working in group means learning new group technique.

Innovation and Change require many kinds of Competences at different point of Work:
Competences need to be organized into effective working team so that all the research works are made available. Who should be involved, at what point? What should be the role of administrators,

curriculum specialist, specialist in group dynamics and research, lay people and students? To develop an adequate use of manifold talent and resources, it is important to practice the principles of level of involvement. Not every type of competences is relevant at every point of curriculum development. Not everyone needs to participate in everything.

Managing Curriculum Innovation Need Skilled Leadership:

It also requires distributed leadership. Issues to be raised at this point are; what are the chief attribute of such leadership? Who can assume each leadership role? What resources in leadership role must the school draw from outside? How should it use these outside consultants? These are but a few strategy for curriculum innovation and change.

Factors that Influence Curriculum Innovation and Change

Curriculum innovation is very vital as it enhances effective quality control mechanism of the school programme by ensuring that the school curriculum stands the test of time. A worthwhile innovation ought to be purposeful. Oteh and Akuma (2010) identify some reasons for curriculum innovation; such as dynamic nature of knowledge, improved teaching and learning, research finding etc. Other factors include changes in societal needs and aspirations, changes in the nature of knowledge, changes in the system of education and outcome of curriculum education evaluation. These factors are discussed as follows:

Changes in Societal Needs and Aspirations:
The school is an agency established to serve the needs of the community. This implies that the character and structure of the curriculum will be determined by the dominant forces at work in the community at any given time. Changes in societal needs naturally call for changes in the objectives of education. For example in Nigeria, during the colonial time, the school curriculum thought not explicit aimed at producing teachers, catechist, and clerks for the local court and as interpreters who will help in preaching the Word of God in addition enhance the growing commercial empire of the Europeans. Such fitted into the general scheme of things as planned by the colonial masters. By the mid of (1960s), it was observed that most of the school leaver could not be employed. The economy was changed. It began to demand skilled manpower. There was a lot of allegation on the school that the school had failed to educate individual to meet the demand of the society. In order words, the objective of education had changed. Hence, the curriculum needed to be changed to meet the new expectation. In effect, the National Curriculum Conference of 1969 organized by the Nigerian Educational Research Council (NERC) was a culmination of the people dissatisfactions of the colonial education. The conference identified new goals of education which

the existing curriculum could not meet. Naturally a curriculum change or innovation has to be under taken. Hence, a major factor which informs curriculum innovation and change is change in societal needs and aspiration.

Changes in the Nature of Knowledge:
Prior to this year, Europe was producing books at a rate of about 1000 titles per year. Today, the American Government have generated over 100,000 report each year in addition to over 4,500 articles, books and papers. The computer which surfaced around 1950 is also another major force behind the latest acceleration in the acquisition of knowledge.

In addition to the above mentioned, research have brought about more avenues for knowledge explosion. E.g. in the area of mathematics, we now have "New Mathematics or Modern Mathematics or even Further Mathematics and statistics", likewise in science, we have integrated science, as well as combinations of branches of science such as Agric, Economics, Bio-Chemistry, Micro-Biology, Geo-Physics among others. These new areas adopt new concept and methodology which unavoidably influence the curriculum. The curriculum need to be modified to take these new subjects, new ways of learning or organizing, learning experience such as computer based learning, teaching machines which amount from researches in education, all exert pressure on the curriculum. It could be right therefore to accept that changes in the content of education constitute factors to be recorded with in bringing about curriculum innovation and change.

Changes in Learning Process:

Recent findings from empirical research in human motivation has suggested means of progressive educational planning of the optimal curriculum with reference to needs, interest, levels of previous experience, abilities and aptitudes of the children seeking education. First, it was a faculty psychology. The associationist sees learning as a process of trial and error. Learning is judged to have occurred when strong S- R bonds have been established as a result of conditioning. Complex skills and habits are learned through the re-enforcement of the many simple SR until that comprises the whole. In general the associationist sees behaviour and learning in terms of mechanical relationship among discrete variables. On the other hand, the field theory or cognitive theory view learning as process of insight i.e. learning is judged to have occurred when the person has experienced a re-structuring of perception otherwise the understanding of the total situation. While the constructivist views learning as a re-construction of previous experience. A good example of psychologist whose theory has changed the curriculum are Piaget and Jerome Brunner. Several curriculum developed in many countries in recent times are evidence of matching curriculum to fit stages of cognitive functioning of learners. For example, Brunner's theory on discovery learning has influenced the organization of instruction mostly in mathematics and the science discipline.

Changes in the System of Education:

In the early 1950's, we had 9 years of primary schooling, 5 years of secondary education and 3 years or more of tertiary education. In the training of teachers there were so many stages which an individual had to scale through before he or she will be regarded as a trained teacher. The stages are:

i.   Pre-Elementary Training Centre (P.T.C)
ii.   Elementary Teachers College (ETC)
iii.   Higher Elementary Teachers College (HETC)

With time, the primary education curriculum was reviewed to last for 6 years. Consequently the curriculum has to be changed. A change in the system of education that ha affected the curriculum was the training of teachers. With the lunching of the universal primary education in September 1976, there was the need for crash programme to mass produce as many teachers as possible for the scheme, hence the duration of teacher training was shortened. Based on the change, comes an innovation in the curriculum so as to emphasis the most important teacher training programme. The introduction of the new education system 6 — 3 — 3 — 4 in Nigeria brought about a thorough innovation and change in our school system.

Outcome of Curriculum Evaluation:

Good curriculum planning requires the planners to set up a machinery for periodic evaluation of the curriculum, such evaluation aim at determining how well the curriculum has achieved the intended goal. The focus of such evaluation may also be on the total impact of the curriculum on the school system including problems and issues related to its adoption or rejection. Data's from such systematic evaluation becomes a factor that could lead to change or revision of the existing Curriculum.

Theories of Innovation and Changes
Scholars at different time have propounded various theories of change and innovation which can be applied to the educational system. Notable among these scholars are Ronald Havelock, Donald Schon and Earnest House. Analyses of each of these theories are provided for a better understanding.

Ronald Havelock Theory of Change
Havelock (1971) after an extensive study on dissemination of innovation concludes that innovation can be grouped according to how their authors view the dissemination and utilization process. Havelock therefore offered three model or theories of innovation such as Problem Solving Model (P- S), Social Interaction Model (S- I) and Research Development and Diffusion Model (RD & D)

Problem Solving Model (P-S):

Individuals or groups in this model, the process of change by identifying an area of concern or by sensing a need for change. Once the problem area is identified, the receiver undertakes to alter the situation either through his own effort, or by recruiting suitable outside assistance. In this situation, the receiver of the innovation in this model is active rather than passive as will be identified in the other two models. From the above analysis, it can be observed that the application of this model is basically controlled by need. The user must have a need for change. This model is also diagnostic as the problem must be identified, and the situation analyzed so as to locate the dimensions of the problems and its causes.

After the analysis has been carried out, alternative solutions are identified. Such solutions are tried out where necessary, and can be modified before final adaption.

The role of outside agent in this model is minimal and merely consultative since his inputs or ideas may or may not be accepted. One of the interesting features of this model is the utilization of local initiative, collaboration, self help and other local resources. This makes it to have a participatory flavour as the user of the innovation is fully committed to his course.

Relating this model to the Nigerian education, shortly after the attainment of independence, it was observed that the Nigerian education was no more relevance to the needs and aspiration of the people. Thus a National Curriculum Conference was called in 1969, which comprised of people from different sectors of the Nigerian society so that they could contribute idea towards the development of Nigerian education. The outcome of the conference led to the emergence of a National Policy on Education called 6 -3 – 3-4 system. In reviewing the educational system, Nigerian also invited foreign agencies such as U.N.E.S.C.O, U.N.D.P and U.N.I.C.E.F Nigeria in this process adopted the problem solving model of curriculum innovation and change.

Strength and Weakness of the Problem Solving Model:
The strengths of the problem solving model as indicated by Nwafor (2007) are as follows:

- ❖ It enhances effective and efficient utilization of available resources including local media.
- ❖ It generates a high level of resources (human and non-human) from within.
- ❖ People are involved in initiating and executing projects to serve their needs.
- ❖ Opportunities for early replacement of any outside resources involved in the projects are allowed.
- ❖ There is maximum utilization of internal resources.

- ❖ There is local commitment due to high level of people's involvement.
- ❖ It has direct relationship with the needs of the users which in turn enhances the relevance of the innovation.

The weakness of the problem solving model are:
- ❖ Poor social relationship that may enhance the effective implementation of the innovation.
- ❖ Bureaucratic problems. For example the delay in the implementation of the recommendation of the 1969 curriculum conference can be associated with this factor.
- ❖ Neglect from political elite. Politics may interfere with the model as such the political elite may decide to abandon it irrespective of its obvious advantages.

Social Interaction Model (S-I):
This model has five main stages namely awareness, interest, evaluation, trial and adaptation. In the first stage, an innovation is presented or brought to the attention of a potential receiver population. The needs of the receivers are determined exclusively by the sender. The receiver is supposed to react to the new information and the nature of his reaction determines whether or not subsequence stages will occur. If his awareness is followed by expression of

interest, he is launched on a series of steps which finally terminates with acceptance or rejection of the innovation. This emphasizes the trial, evaluation and adaptation stages.

The diffusion of the innovation depends greatly upon the channel of communication between the receivers and the senders groups, since the information about the innovation is transmitted primarily through the social interaction of the group members and the sequence of implementation may be-truncated by rejection at any stage. For example, the innovation in the Nigerian health sector; the reaction (negative) of some Northern State to the National Immunization Programme for children against the child killer diseases such as polio, measles, tuberculoses, tetanus, whooping cough, chicken pox, among others. They claimed that immunization will cause infertility to the beneficiary. But their prominent leaders both political and religious had to intervene. Likewise, some individual and religious groups kicked against the use of condom as a preventive measure against sexually transmistted diseases (S.T.Ds) Here again, interaction is provided through the media, group campaign and enlightenment seminars.

Authors who consider the process of innovation from the above point of view are concerned with the stages through which individuals pass as they reach a decision to adopt an innovation. In addition, they are concerned with the related issue of the mechanism by which the innovation diffuses through the adopting group. Studies in this area have shown that the most effective means of information is through personal contact. Thus, the key to adaptation is viewed by authors of this school or model, to be social interaction among members of the adopting group.

Some of the major characteristics of the social interaction model are as follows:

- ❖ The individual user is a member of a social group which can influence his or her behaviour.
- ❖ The position of the individual tries to predict the rate of his or her acceptance of new ideas.
- ❖ Information personal/group contacts are important to convince people to accept and adopt the innovation.
- ❖ The rate of the diffusion starts slowly and subsequently speeds up.
- ❖ Group membership is a predictor of the individual adoption.

The social interaction model is important in the fact that it allows for easy replacement of any form of outside resources used for the innovation. It accommodates locally — initiated innovations which are more strongly related to the problems of the people than foreign ideas. The feeling is that if the strategy is used by National agencies, it is capable of attracting national government contribution to resources, and the capability of evaluating it is greatly enhanced.

On the contrary, this model has been questioned because it was researched based on the diffusion of agricultural innovations such as hybrid corn or the introduction of fertilizers in farming. The educational systems are not comparable farms and farmers unlike the educational innovations, agricultural innovations are easily evaluated visibly and reliably. Similarly, emphasis is placed on the early chases of change awareness and adaptation rather than implementation stage which is the major stumbling block in education. Other problem of the model include focus on the individual to bring about change as opposed to institution and difficulty involved for either opinion leaders or political leaders to influence other people to adapt an innovation in an educational system, especially if a major change is expected.

Research Development and Diffusion Model (RD & D):
This model is based on the assumption that reform follows an orderly sequence which begins with the research development, diffusion and finally to the dissemination of the solution to the target group. The research development and diffusion perspective looks at the process of change from the point of view of the originator of an innovation and it begins with the formulation of the problem on the basis of a

presumed receiver need. The initiative in making this identification however is taken by the developers not the one receiving and in this way, the RD & D model is similar to the S –I model. However, that it views the process of change from an earlier point in time. The focus is on the activities phases of the developer as he designs and develops a potential solution to a problem he has identified. The initiative in these activities is taken by the researcher, the developers and disseminators, the receiver remains essentially perceive.

The major emphasis of all the theories in the RD & D School is on the planning of a change on a large scale. These involved detailed development based on scientific knowledge and rigorous testing and evaluation. It also involves mechanism for distributing the information to its target group. For example, in the educational practice, teaching methods are chosen, appropriate teaching materials devised, tried out and revised are necessary. The final stage of the change continuum involves the diffusion of the new idea to local areas for adaptation.

America and Britain adapted this model during her curriculum reform movement to restructure their educational system aimed at producing the needed scientist that will challenge the scientific breakthrough of the former Soviet Union (U.S.S.R). In Nigeria, this model was adapted by the former Bendel State in the development and implantation of curriculum for all the former Bendel State owned Colleges of Education with a central curriculum development center 'at Abraka. At present, this model is adapted by the National Teachers Institute (NTI), National Open University of Nigeria and National Commission for Colleges of Education (NCCE) in the implementation of its programme. These bodies have a Central Curriculum Development Centres that design the curriculum for its agencies and enforce its adaptation in the school system with little or no modification.

Strength and Weakness of the RD & D Model

❖ It reduces cost by reducing the error that could have been incurred without initial trial.

❖ It makes for effective utilization of human resources who are usually drawn to the centre and charged with the responsibilities of researching, developing and disseminating innovation.

❖ Its system approach or scientific approach gives or guarantee for high level of validity, reliability and usability.

❖ It has the advantage of showing the changes process in a logical order from discovery to utilization.

❖ The innovation can get a very wide audience due to its publications and large scale production of required materials.

- ❖ The dissemination stages make it easy for teachers to understand how to adapt the innovation.
- ❖ It promises continuity of relevance.

Disadvantages of RD & D Model
- ❖ Its predominant use discourages local initiatives and originality of local people.
- ❖ Intended users may lack the necessary knowledge and skills if care is not taken.
- ❖ Local needs and variation can be neglected.
- ❖ The level of research activities cannot be guaranteed.
- ❖ The necessary research level such as summative and formative evaluations are often omitted.

Donald Schon Theory of Change (Three Models for Diffusion)

Schon has taken models for diffusion beyond the assumption embedded in previous models. In his presentations, Schon considers the survival requirement of social system entering a phase of permanent change and articulate a code of public learning appropriate to such systems.

In the course of his analysis, he examined models for the diffusion of innovation taking a view of social change which has the outward spread of inventions as its key explanatory idea. Schon himself put the main point neatly:

> *"Diffusion of innovation is a dominant model for the transformation of societies according to which novalty moves out from one or more points to permeate the society as a whole"*

Schon's influence on contemporary theory of curriculum change has been pervasive in the field of education, as stated below.

The Centre-Periphery Model:
This model rest on the first of Schon's model is the three basic assumptions; that the innovation exists fully realized in its essentials, prior to its diffusion that diffusion is the movement of an innovation from a centre out to its ultimate users, that directed diffusion is a centrally managed process of dissemination, training and the provision of resources and incentives.

The effectiveness of a. centrally periphery system depends among other things on the level of resources at the centre, the number of points at the periphery, length of the spokes through which diffusion takes place and the energy needed to gain a new adoption. It might be felt that "spoke length is a rather feeble and un-enlightened metaphor and Schon does not repeat it, talking instead of infrastructural technology and maintaining that the scope of centre periphery system varies directly and with the length of technology governing the flow means, materials, money and information. The scope also depends upon the systems capacity for generating and managing feedback. Because the process of diffusion is regulated by the centre, its effectiveness depends upon the ways in which information flows back to the centre.

Simple systems of this kind are prone to failure says Schon, through resources exhaustion, overload and mismanagement. When the centre periphery system, exist the resource or the energy at the centre over loads the capacity of the radio, or mishandles feedback from the periphery it fails. Failure takes the form of simple ineffectiveness in diffusion, distortion of the message or disintegration of the system as a whole.

The Proliferation Model:
Schon depicts his second model of diffusion process and call it the "Proliferation Centre Model". It is a suggestion Schon designed as though to extend the limits and overcome the sources of failure inherent in the simpler model. This system retains the basic centre periphery structure that differentiates primary and secondary centre. The secondary centres engage in the diffusion of innovation, primary centres support and manages secondary centre. The effect is to multiply and reach the efficiency of the diffusion system. In this "model, the proliferation of the secondary centres provides a re-

enforcement to the action of the centre which its new centre creates its own periphery and infrastructure. The limit to the reach and effectiveness of the system depends now on the primary centres ability to generate, support and manage the new centres. The model of the proliferation of centres makes for the primary centre a trainer of trainers. The central massage includes not only the content of the innovation to be diffused but a pre-established method for its diffusion. The primary centres now specialize in training, development, supporting monitoring and management.

Schon describes the content of industrial expansion, the dominant pattern in the primary centre relationship to the secondary centres as follows:

*   The primary centre is a guardian of pre-established doctrine and methodology. It selects territories for expansion and deploys and organizes agents of expansions.

*   It is not only the source and model of operation to be diffused but the developers of methodology of diffusion.

*   It trains and incubates new agents of diffusion.

*   It supports de-centralized outputs through capital, information and know-how.

*   It monitors and manages de-centralized operations, certain criteria or performance monitoring performance, observance and overseeing leadership is the outpost.

*   It maintains information throughout the next work of outpost.

The sources of failure in the proliferation of the centre mode are similar to those in the main mode. The demand in the central management, particularly the central doctrine may not meet the needs of secondary centre leaders looking for support and flexibility to counter local resistance and such centres may become detached from the primary centre. When that happens, the diffusion system fragments and becomes unable to maintain itself except may still transform in special societies but the information no longer consists in the diffusion of an established message. It leads readers to a variety of regional transformation which bears only a family resemblance to one another.

The effectiveness of this approach depends to a large extent on the ability of primary centres to generate support and manage auxiliary centres. A major source of its failure concerns limited infrastructure, technology and other human and material resources. Infact, when the network of communication, money, men, information and materials are inadequate to the demand imposed on

111

it, the innovation suffers a setback sometimes ending in a total failure. Example is the failure of the technical arm of the 6- 3- 3 -4 system of education.

Periphery - Centre or the Shifting Centre Model:
This model is in reverse direction to the centre — periphery. This is the "shifting centre" model which Schon argues is a characteristic of contemporary social movement which operates in groups within an established organization. This model does not suffer from dependant on limited resources and competency and from rigidity of central doctrine. Problems are first encountered at the "initial stage" if it appears that reform is needed, such information is disseminated to the central organization which makes suggestion about how localized and solutions may be reached. Schon defines its characteristics as a system of diffusion in the following terms.

Characteristics of the Periphery — Centre Model

❖ The model has no clearly established centre. The centres appear reach a peak and disappear to be replaced by new centres within a short period of time.

❖ This model does not have a stabled centrally established message. The messages shifts and involves producing a family of related messages.

❖ The system of movement in this model cannot be described as centre
periphery. The centre rise and fall. Messages also change based on the model of the

112

receivers. But movement is a diffusing learning system in which both primary and secondary messages evolves rapidly along the organization of diffusion itself.

All these are made possible by technology of modern communication system which enable participants in the movement to have continuous access through the media, telephone, and rapid transport systems to the present of its flexible structure. The model can be regrouped around new centres. Adhoc leadership is by those who articulate the latest move, and cannot be maintained for long because the leaders, cannot control or monopolize the information on which centre pies for leadership will be based. They do not have time to change the social network into an organization without such-contro1 before a new transformation occurs.

Earnest House Theory of Change (Diffusion in Urban Societies)

House is the most recent of the theorist to be considered. His focus is firmly on educational innovation and to a large extent arises out of personal experiences of the curriculum reform movement. He is able to take into account nearly a decade of attempts to implement one major variant of the centre — periphery model, the Research Development and Diffusion (RD & D) first identified by Havelock.

Although he offers no new model of innovation diffusion. House takes the theory of "personal contact" which derived largely from studies of innovation in Rural Societies and updates it, showing how some characteristics phenomena of urbanization such as changes in transportation, population distribution and social group structure, impact on the functioning of the process in the field of educational innovation.

The Rural population or community is homogenous in nature so that contagious diffusion (one person talking to another person similar in social status) is the rule. In such cases, the major factor limiting personal contact and hence innovation is distance. House contrast this with the urban society "as urbanization increases, population density shift and become more heterogeneous; barriers such as social status becomes more significant than distance in impending personal communication".. Here, House contends that the pattern of spread change; instead of regular waves emerging from fixed points as in rural diffusion innovation elapsed from one concentration of population to the next largest in size. Independent of distance. House calls this the "urban hierarchy" of distribution and although the pattern does not exclude some "contagious" diffusion, it exercise and predominate over distance.

The problem for innovation diffusion House argues is how to extend the contact network of teachers and breakdown the barriers that prevent the formation of personal contact networks that cuts across levels of the educational hierarchy. Both horizontal transmission by teachers and vertical transmission ministrators are seriously impended by such barriers. A more effective approach to educational change, House argues would take account of the urban hierarchy, promoting rapid adoption in the larger regional centres, provides more incentives for local entrepreneurs and increasing the number participating in the changed enterprise. Above all, the aim should be to reduce political, social and organizational barriers to contact the outside world. It is in the nature of organizations to limit such involvement. Giving teachers access to the outside personal contacts that administrators now have would tremendously increase innovation diffusion in education. General urban development will also assist in the process.

Strategies for Innovation and Change
The general goal of the change agent is to develop strategies for bringing about change. Those strategies have been divided into three major types, such as

The Empirical — Rational Strategy:
This strategy assumes that people are rational i.e. they can think and that they will act on the basis of the best information available. Therefore in order to improve people ability to make decisions, one needs only to present them with the facts. Basically, the strategy in making innovation process with research

and development, with emphasis have been place on dialogue between the consumer and innovation. In it, as in Schon centre-periphery model and Havelock's R, D & D models, change is proposed by expert such as educational administrators (acting at the centre) who are assumed to understand its effects on the individual, group or organization. Communication is largely one- way process. It is from people who know (the innovators) to those who do not know (users).

The professional role demanded by the empirical-rational strategy has been described as that of an analyst — i.e. one who tries objectively to diagnose a problem and to bring appropriate data to bear units solution. There has probably been more demand for the analyses role than any other; moreover this role has been popular among social psychologists. Most of the Governmental research is based on the empirical rational strategy - i.e. Governmental Agencies Fund Research that will produce facts, which can then be disseminated for the purpose of affecting change. The empirical rational strategy is limited in that no guarantee exists as to what kind of people will read the information or put it to use.

The Normative - Re-Educative Strategy:
The normative re-educative strategy assumes that people are intelligent and rational, but it also assumes that they are bound up in their own particular centre. As a result; they have definite behavioural responses and patterns that are based

on attitudes, values, traditions and relationships with others. Before trying to change a person, group or community, these cultural or normative determinants must be taken into account. This strategy assumes that change will occur only as individuals involved in the process are made to change their normative orientations to old patterns and develop commitments to new ones. Such re-orientation involves change in the know-how, knowledge, skills, values, etc. In this strategy, image of the client is that of cooperation. Communication is a two-way process. The change agent is open to influence just as he is likely to influence the receiver system.

The normative - re-educative model is particularly useful were the objective of the innovation is to change teachers attitude, opinion towards students, colleague or curriculum methods. Educational inspectors, advisers, consultants and all those whose jobs involves changing peoples awareness or improving interpersonal relationships might also find it useful.

The Power — Coercive Strategy:
This strategy is based on political, economic, and social uses of power that have been most popular and effective in bringing about change. Under this strategy, change is initiated by elected politicians who use the law of government directives as a medium. In education, it is used to pass laws against certain activities or to ensure order.

Nevertheless, the power — coercive strategy are seldom sufficient change method in and of themselves. The power — coercive approach must be coupled with the normative re-educative approach to maximize change. Legal sanctions established the letter of the law but normative re-educative strategy fosters the spirit of the law. It is one thing to declare that change must take place, it is quite another to build the social mechanisms attitudes and relationships that will actually produce these changes with a minimum of disruption.

Summary and Conclusion
In this chapter we have examined the concept of curriculum innovation and change. The chapter also takes a look at the various aspects of curriculum change and innovation relative to some curriculum innovation projects. Theories of innovations was examined relative to the works of Have Lock, Earnest House and Donald Schon. The chapter therefore concludes that curriculum innovation and change is crucial as it makes the school programme stand the taste of time.

CHAPTER FIVE

CURRICULUM IMPLEMENTATION AND INSTRUCTION

INTRODUCTION

In one of the previous chapter of this book, we examined the process of developing a school curriculum. One of the stages so identified in this regard was the stage of curriculum implementation. To this view we explained that curriculum implementation involves the classroom effort of teachers and student in putting into operation what is obtained in the curriculum document. In such analysis, the teachers' role was also examined as he is the key factor that determines the direction and effectiveness of the implementation process of any school curriculum. To this effect therefore, this chapter will examine among others the concept of curriculum implementation, teaching and instruction, process of curriculum implementation, factors that influences curriculum implementation and instruction and lastly problems of implementing school curriculum in Nigeria.

What Is Curriculum Implementation?

In chapter one of this work, many definitions of the concept curriculum have been given, ranging from its historical connotation, narrow and broad perspectives. Curriculum in all ramifications means all the desirable learning experience brought to the learner under the auspices of the school for the learners personal growth and positive contributions towards the development of the society. This implies that curriculum is implemented in the school. As implemented in school, there are key actors involved in such implementation process, which include the teacher, learners and other stakeholders in the school system. Thus, in examining the concept of curriculum implementation these actors must be involved. Thus, curriculum implementation is the actual engagement of learners with planned learning opportunities. Curriculum implementation stage is the stage when in the midst of learning activities, teachers and learners are involved in negotiation aimed at promoting learning. At this stage the teacher adopts the appropriate teaching methods and resources to guide learning. The learners on their own are actively involved in the process of interaction with learning activities. Offorma (2005) explains that curriculum implementation is the transmission of the planned curriculum into the operational curriculum. Jeremiah (2004) states that at the curriculum implementation stage teachers are involved in drawing out the lesson plan from the scheme of work, identification and selection of appropriate instructional methods and materials to use, classroom management, proper evaluation of instructional content and actual teaching. Thus curriculum implementation can be regarded as the actual interaction between the teacher and the learners aimed at achieving stated objectives as may be obtained in the lesson plan.

What is teaching?

Over the years, scholars have given different definitions of the concept of teaching in different ways. Saylor, Alexander and Lanes (1981) explained that teaching is a process whereby one person mediates between one another with the substance of his world to facilitate learning. A major problem in this definition is that it makes everybody a teacher. Anybody can help another person learn something but that does not make that person a teacher. Teaching in educational perspectives, may be conceived as a profession or as the activities engaged in by those who belong to that profession. In this regard, teaching differs from what goes on in the church, family and other social groups.

Another scholar Pring (1972,) defines teaching as engaging in certain activities which you have ground to believe will be instrumental in bringing about in another person the learning of something that can be characterized or specified. The above definition of teaching contains two important criteria for teaching namely: intent and means. This implies that the person doing the teaching has some objective or intention and he utilizes appropriate resources for doing that. However this definition has not placed teaching in the right perspective of its professional standard. It still presents it as something anybody can do and as having to do with any content. Education is concerned with worthwhile knowledge, skills, values, beliefs aimed at preparing the individual for a useful life in the society. If intent and means .used as the major variables of teaching then setting up activities to enable somebody learn how to carryout kidnapping activities can be classified as teaching. It is important to note that this type of knowledge cannot be classified as worthwhile.

Teaching therefore involve setting up of activities to enable somebody learn something which can improve persons knowledge, skill, attitudes and value. Thus, Akinkpelu (1981) averrs that teaching is a deliberate effort by a mature or experienced person to impart information, knowledge, skills and so on to an immature or less experienced person through a process that is normally and pedagogically acceptable. According to Akinkpelu, the content of teaching has to be worthwhile and the procedure has to be educationally acceptable for an activity to be classified as teaching. The aim of any teaching encounter is to facilitate learning.

Ibe-Bassey (2002), contend that teaching is a systematic, rational and organized process of translating knowledge, skills, attitude and value in accordance with certain professional principles. This observation implies that teaching can only be carried out in an organized process with certain professional principles. To this effect, therefore Ibe-Bassey looked at teaching on a professional perspective because such organized process can only be manipulated by a trained teacher. All that teaching does is to set up the necessary condition of learning of that which is intended. Since teaching is an intentional act, there is need to know when the intention has been achieved. Teaching does not end at sending the message, it also ensure adequate feedback. Teaching can therefore be defined as a programme of activities aimed at inculcating desirable learning experiences by a trained teacher to the learner through a prescribed methodological approach. The implication of this definition is many sided. In the first instance, it implies that what is taught and what the learner learn must be desirable to the learner and the society. It also implies that such act can only be carried out by a professional teacher who has the requisite skill or knowledge in the act of teaching. Lastly, the definition also implies that teaching goes with prescribed methodological or instructional approach. The act of teaching is not carried out indiscriminately rather it follows some prescribed methodologies or strategies. This justifies the reason why we have various teaching strategies that can be applied at different point in time taking into consideration some fundamental variables. Jeremiah (2009) outlines such variables as specific learning objectives, subject matter, the learner, resource materials, classroom size, comfort of the learning environment and time.

What is instructing?
The teachers role at the curriculum implementation stage is many sided which involves drawing out the scheme of work from the syllabus, closely followed by unit plan and lesson plan and finally presenting

the lesson to learners as stated in the lesson plan. At this stage, the teacher comes in close contact with the learner to implement his decision. At this point, the teacher sets up different activities, adopt various strategies and technique to achieve the desired change in learners behaviour. Thus all the activities engaged by the teacher with the aim of facilitating change in learners' behaviour can be classified as instruction. Instruction can therefore be conceived as the planned interaction between the learner and the learning activities. It is through this interaction that learning occurs.

Offorma (1994) explains that instruction is the hypotheses testing stage. At the planning stage, the teacher is formulating hypotheses regarding his intended action and those of the learners. The testing art of this hypotheses constitute instruction. During instruction, the teacher is putting his plans and theories into practice. He modifies his plans and strategies to suit a given class environment. He observes learners behaviour and learning styles to get feedback. Such feedback provides a basis to adjust his instructional strategies when the teacher engages in such activities with the aim of promoting learning, he is instructing.

Instruction is the last phase of curriculum implementation stage. It involves the class interaction between the teacher and the learner aimed at achieving the objectives of a particular learning. Activities involved at the instructional stage include: effective classroom management, identification of learning problems of the learner, uses and application of appropriate instructional materials and methods and proper evaluation procedure.

Process of Curriculum Implementation And Instruction

The process of curriculum implementation and instruction involves certain steps which will include analysis of the curriculum, syllabus, scheme of work and lesson plan. A proper analysis of each of these concepts relative to curriculum implementation is made below.

Curriculum

In the earlier part of this work, a proper analysis of the concept of curriculum was made. One of the definitions captured explained that curriculum is all the desirable learning experience brought to the learner under the auspices of the school for the learners personal growth and positive contributions towards the development of the society. Sources of the school curriculum include the learner, the society, national philosophy, the teacher, professional organization, subject specialist and the layman. These bodies or organizations exact some pressure on the school curriculum which makes it to change with time. A school curriculum must also posses some unique characteristics. Some of these characteristics according to NTI (2009) include purposeful aims and objectives, functionality, flexibility, relevance and evaluation. While the major component of a school curriculum as earlier noted in this work include programme of studies, programme of activities and programme of guidance.

Syllabus

The syllabus is the second important concept to be examined on the process of curriculum implementation and instruction. Jeremiah (2009) noted that the syllabus specified all that should be studied in each subject for the period the learner is in the school within a particular level of education. This implies that we may have nursery school syllabus, primary school syllabus, secondary school syllabus or tertiary education syllabus. The syllabus is the programme of study component of the school curriculum. Sometimes, it is called minimum standard or even prospectus. In Nigeria, various bodies are responsible for the provision of school syllabus. Such bodies include West African Examination Council (WAEC), National Examination Council (NECO), Universal Basic Education Commission (UBEC), National Teachers Institute (NTI), and Federal Ministry of Education (FME). These bodies are either classified as examination bodies or administrative machinery responsible for the affairs of education within a particular level. In recent times, innovation trend has included certain elements in the syllabus such elements are topics, performance objective, content, instructional materials, methodology, evaluation. Such arrangement according to Jeremiah (2004) makes it

126

easier for teachers to analyze properly the content area of the syllabus for effective implementation of the school curriculum. We have two types of syllabus such as teaching and examination syllabus.

Scheme of Work

When the syllabus gets to the school from the various bodies, there is the need to split or reduce it into a manageable portion on yearly, termly and weekly basis. This implies that if there are, for instance forty topics for primary four Social Studies, about twelve topics should be studied every term, relative to the number of terms obtained in the academic year. One important issue about the scheme of work is that it is designed by the school teacher. It is at this point that the teacher brings into bear his professional knowledge. The teacher at this point can modify the scheme of work to suit local conditions or local needs. Thus by drawing out the scheme of work, teachers are given the opportunity to contribute their idea on the issue of curriculum development and implementation. In more simple terms, the scheme of work contains information, about what the learner is expected to learn on yearly, termly and weekly basis.

Other important information that can be obtained in the scheme of work include: record of work, summary of students result, head teacher's comment, recommended text and general note.

Lesson Plan

When the scheme of work has been drawn, the teacher plans the lesson by writing a lesson plan for each topic or sub-topics in the scheme of work. Thus the lesson plan consist of these specific learning activities which evolves from a given unit concept. Each lesson plan is structured around a problem specifically designed to guide the process of reflective thinking. A lesson plan is also the systematic organization of a content of the unit course in such a manner that it will guide teachers to achieve effective instruction. It can also be referred to as an outline of essential experience which the teacher wants the pupils to acquire. A lesson plan also contain step by step information that guide the teacher on how to present an instructional content.

Jeremiah (2009) further defines the lesson plan as a well thought out, orderly and sequential arrangement of lesson on paper, it names the subject matter, state the objectives and describe the part both the learner and the teacher will play in the course of the lesson in order to achieve a given objective. Jeremiah further stated that education is yet to evolve a universally acceptable format or model of writing a lesson plan. Some teachers may present their lesson plan using the essay format while others may use the tabular format. Other may use the conventional model, or T.K.T model or constructivist model or any other model they may be conversant with. Whichever model or format used, such a lesson plan should be accepted provided certain elements are obtained in the plan. These elements are discussed in relation to the given model of presenting a lesson plan.

Process of curriculum implementation

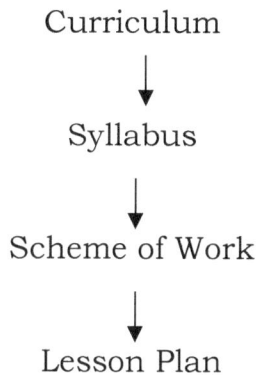

Curriculum

↓

Syllabus

↓

Scheme of Work

↓

Lesson Plan

Fig. 3 **Process of curriculum implementation**

Parts of a Lesson Plan (Conventional Model)
The conventional model of lesson planning refers to the tradition approach of lesson presentation which teachers are used to for ages.

This approach seems to have a direct relationship with the objective model of curriculum design as advocated by Raif Tyler, D.K. Wheeler, and Dennis Lawton. More specifically, the traditional model of lesson plan borrows its elements from the work of Tyler. Tyler (1950) in his Basic Principles of Curriculum and Instruction identifies four steps of

129

curriculum development process which includes objectives, selection of learning experience, organization of learning experience and lastly evaluation. The conventional model of lesson planning starts with the formulation of objectives which terminates with evaluation. At this stage we will examine the various parts of a conventional lesson plan. Jeremiah and Vipene (2013) identify the various parts of a conventional lesson plan as follows:

- ❖ Preamble
- ❖ Specific Objectives
- ❖ Entry Behaviour
- ❖ Set Induction
- ❖ Teachers Activities
- ❖ Pupils Activities
- ❖ Resource Materials
- ❖ Methodology
- ❖ Chalkboard Summary
- ❖ Evaluation Procedure

Each of these parts of the conventional lesson plans are discussed below.

❖ **Preamble**:
The preamble is the first part of a conventional lesson plan. It contain information about the subject, topic of the lesson, number of students or pupils in the class, gender, age, name of school, number of periods, location of school and other

related issues. In a survey conducted by one of the authors in 2010, it was observed that most teachers in Nigerian schools do not know the implication of the preamble as a part of lesson plan. They believe that it is just a routine activity to write the preamble as part of their lesson plan. The preamble is very important as it gives the head teacher, or supervisors of school or any other evaluator a first hand knowledge or information about what he is expected to observe or see in the lesson. For example, in a situation whereby a teacher has indicated that he has about 105 pupils in a particular arm of the primary class.

The implication is that such a teacher may probably encounter the problem of classroom management. On this note therefore, supervisor of such instruction may play down on this problem when they arise within the instructional process.

❖ **Specific Objectives**

Specific objectives under instructional point of view are also called behavioural objectives or instructional objectives. This relates to what the students are expected to achieve at the end of the lesson. They are the expected behavioural outcome of the learner at the end of the instructional process. Such objectives are always stated in behavioural terms using action verbs. For example in Basic One Mathematics using the topic "Simple Fraction", the specific objective may be captured as follows:

By end of the lesson, pupils should be able to:
i.   Demonstrate with practical examples the meaning of simple fraction
ii.   Identify three simple fractions

Jeremiah (2009) indicates some qualities of a good specific objective as follows:

- ❖ Objectives must be started in behavioural terms
- ❖ Specific objectives must be stated with action verbs
- ❖ A good specific objective must be measurable
- ❖ Specific objective must take into consideration the various domain of Education.
- ❖ A good objective must take into consideration the developmental level of the learner
- ❖ Such objectives must have a direct relationship with the evaluation process.

❖ Entry Behaviour

The use of entry behaviour in lesson planning has created a lot of confusion in the field of instructional strategies. Some scholars use the word previous knowledge rather than entry behaviour. It is on this note that Jeremiah (2009) observes that "teachers are often confused on the word entry behaviour, and previous knowledge. Previous knowledge on its own relates to the totality of all the knowledge or experiences that the child has that will enable such child understand the lesson or topic to be taught. Such knowledge may be too diverse as such in writing the lesson plan we use entry behaviour instead of previous knowledge". Entry behaviour implies the specific knowledge the learner has that can be drawn or utilized by the teacher that will enhance proper achievement of the learner. Hence, entry behaviour is more specific than previous knowledge. For example in the teaching of the topic "fraction", for Basic I Class, the entry behaviour may be "children have been sharing things".

❖ **Set Induction**

Set induction is a teaching skill which a trained teacher is supposed to master and apply effectively in the instructional process. Jeremiah and Job (2011) explains that the concept of set induction may have some link or relationship with what is obtained in the clinical science. More specifically, it can be compared to a situating whereby patients are made to be ready through the process before a surgical operation could be carried out. Without such, the patient may resist the action of the medical officer which will lead to non accomplishment of the task.

In the teaching learning situation, the teacher is the medical officer, while the learner is the patient. Before a teacher will present any instructional content in the classroom situation, he should remember that the learners come to the class from different backgrounds and also the school environments in which learning takes place are indicator of variables that may also effect learners' disposition to learn. As such a good teacher must look for ways to set induce the learners for proper instructional delivery. This has to do with capturing the attention of the pupils, preparing their minds and above all motivating them to receive the new knowledge presented to them. This has to be carried out naturally and spontaneously. The totality of this process according to Singh (2008) is the introduction, but the technical skill used in doing this is set induction.

Keziah (2007) reports that in the teaching learning process, set induction is pre-instructional skill employed by the teacher to arouse and sustain learners' interest and attention. It is a concept that can be described as the brainchild of research findings. The findings of such research indicate that activities carried out before the instructional delivery has a significant effect on students performance.

Jeremiah (2009) contended that set induction is the introduction to the lesson. It is the link between entry behaviour and the lesson. A good set induction must be short and stimulating. Jeremiah, further stated that the main objective of set induction is to arouse learners interest for the incoming lesson. Amajirionwu (1985) sees set induction as a pre-planned action by the teacher to arouse the interest of his students, to create an atmosphere of curiosity and motivation in a classroom and thereby energises, direct and sustains the learners' interest throughout the lesson. In view of the above, set induction can be described as a skill used by the teacher to induce learners to learn. It intensifies excitement and eagerness to perform on the part of the learner. Thus Jeremiah (2009) again concludes that if interest of the learner is not properly aroused, it may be impossible to achieve the objective of a particular lesson. In a lesson plan, set induction can take the form of question and answer, revision of previous lesson and short but related story and classroom exercise or drill mostly at the junior levels of education, it can also take the form of advance ogranizers.

❖ **Teacher's Activity**

Teacher's activity is also called content development. It relates to the sequential organization of the lesson by the teacher. Teacher activities in some lesson plan can also be regarded as development or presentation. This is the stage in a lesson whereby the teacher brings into bear his knowledge about the content area of the subject and topic relative to the objectives of the lesson. At this point, the instructional content is arranged in phases, steps, stages or periods each of which tends to tackle a problem raised in the statement of objectives. For example, if a lesson plan contains three objectives, it implies that the teacher's activities or content development will not be less than three steps. The implication is that each step provides a solution or explains the problem so raised in the statement of objective. A good content development must have a direct relationship with the statement of objectives and the evaluation procedure.

❖ Pupils/Students Activities

As the teacher presents the lesson in the class or through any other media, the learners are expected to react or respond to the instructional process. Such response or reactions of the learner towards the instructional process can be regarded to as student activities. Jeremiah (2009) contends that in the teaching learning process, learners are expected to be active not passive. Thus the students activities is the interactions of the students that will lead to the achievement of the objectives of the lesson. Students activities varies relative to the subject, topic, methods, instructional materials used, evaluation procedure and above all the development characteristics of the learner. Students activities in a lesson can take the form of asking and responding to question, writing down note, laboratory/workshop practice, demonstration of activities etc. Good student activities make the learners to be actively involved in the instructional process thus, enhancing achievement and retention.

❖ Resource Materials

A good lesson plan must also indicate the instructional resource used in teaching the topic. Resource materials in this context are those concrete things the teacher utilizes in presenting his instructional content for effective achievement of the lesson objectives. Resource materials are also called instructional materials. They are the resources used by the teacher in the teaching learning process with the aim of achieving the objectives of the lesson. Such instructional material may be classified as audio, visual and audio-visual materials. Effective application and utilization of instructional materials in a lesson make the learner to participate actively in the instructional process, by so doing enhances achievement and retention.

❖ Methodology

A lesson plan must also state the methods used in presenting such a lesson. Method under instructional point of view can be described as the general process or procedure used by the teacher in organizing the teaching learning process so as to achieve the objectives of a particular lesson. Teaching methods are so called because of the dominant activities involved when, using them. For example, the discussion method is called because of dominant activities involved while using it is discussion. In classroom instruction, teaching methods are not applied indiscriminately. Teacher must consider certain variables for its effective application. Such variables according to Jeremiah (2009) include, specific learning objectives, the learner, subject matter, resource materials, classroom space, comfort of the learning environment and time. A good teacher should consider these factors and others in identifying appropriate teaching method to apply in the instructional process.

❖ Chalkboard Summary

The chalkboard summary is another significant aspect of a conventional lesson plan. It relates to the summary of the lesson that the teacher writes for the learners on the board. It can also be described as the lesson note. This implies that it is the summary of the basic concept taught by the teacher in the class which the learners are made to copy into their notebook. For example a lesson plan for SS I students on the subject "Government" with arms of government as its topic may not explain in details the various arms of government and their functions in the content development segment of the lesson plan. Such detail can be explained in the chalkboard summary. Jeremiah (2009) cautions that the chalkboard summary of a lesson plan should be short but related to content and objectives of the lesson. Jeremiah further explained that wrong application of the chalkboard summary may make nonsense of the lesson plan. To avoid this, un-skillful teacher may avoid the use of chalkboard summary as its absence may not create any significant difference or effect in the lesson plan.

❖ Evaluation Procedure

As earlier explained, evaluation is the last step or stage of the conventional lesson plan. Evaluation under instructional point of view can be described as the systematic process or procedure of knowing the extent by which instructional objectives are achieved. It therefore implies that the evaluation process in a lesson plan must have a direct relationship with the specific objectives. Another important factor to consider is the developmental characteristics of the learner. This implies that any evaluation instrument used must consider the level of the learner. In lesson planning, teacher can utilize oral questions, written question, homework, class work, observation or any other instrument in evaluating students' instructional outcome.

Parts of a Lesson Plan (T.K.T) Model
The Cambridge Teaching Knowledge Task (T.K.T) model of lesson plan is another innovation in the Instructional delivery system. This model of lesson planning is more popular in Rivers State as it was introduced by the former Governor of the State Hon. Rotimi Amechi. For now, no much research work have been conducted on this model of lesson planning. But a survey conducted by Jeremiah (2013) indicates that most teachers in Rivers State don't know the full meaning of the T.K.T model talk of (talk less of) implication of the various segment of the lesson plan in the instructional delivery procedure. This segment of the paper examines the various parts of the T.K.T model of lesson plan which include; preamble, timetable fit, main aim, subsidiary aim, personal aim, assumption, anticipated problems, possible solution,

instructional materials, procedure, interactive pattern, pupils evaluation, teachers evaluation, summary, home work. Each of these segment is examined below.

Preamble

In the T.K.T model, the preamble also form the first part of the lesson plan. It includes information such as the subject, lesson plan heading, number and levels of the learners, etc. It also provide a first hand information to school supervisors or head teacher about what they are expected to see or observe in the lesson.

Timetable Fit

Fit is the introductory part of the T.K.T model of lesson plan. It can be compared to the entry behaviour effect of the conventional lesson plan which involved the specific knowledge learners has acquired that will enable them understand better the topic the teacher intend to teach.

Main Aim

The T.K.T model of lesson plan utilizes the word aim rather than objective. This according to Jeremiah (2013) is one of the major setbacks of this model of lesson plan. Aims are long term target which cannot be achieved with a given instructional period. The main aim in the T.K.T model is always stated in personal terms.

Subsidiary Aim

The subsidiary aim of the T.K.T model of lesson plan is the same with specific objectives in the conventional model which means the expected behavioural outcome of the learner at the end of the instructional process.

Personal Aim

Personal aim is also another segment of T.K.T model of lesson plan. This component has to do with the effective characteristics of the learner. It is not also stated in specific or behavioural terms.

Assumption

Assumption in the T.K.T model of lesson planning relates to the background knowledge of the learner that may be useful for the proper understanding of the new topic the teacher intends to teach. Assumption in this regard may be compared to set induction as obtained in the conventional lesson plan.

Anticipated Problems

The T.K.T model of lesson plan also provides channel to identify the likely problems the learner may encounter on the process of learning the new topic. Such anticipated problems are based on personal assumption by the teacher. On the process of implementing or teaching the topic such assumption may be true or wrong. Thus they can be described as hypothetic models in the lesson plan.

Possible Solution

The possible solution as a segment of the T.K.T model of lesson plan provides strategies in which the anticipated problems will be solved during the instructional delivery process.

Instructional Materials
The T.K.T model of lesson plan also specified the type of instructional materials that will be used in presenting the instructional content just as in the case of conventional method as earlier explained in this chapter.

Procedure
Procedure can be described as the content development, which is the stage in which the instructional content is broken down into phases, unit or period with each providing a solution to the problems raised in the statement of objectives.

Interactive Pattern
This segment of the T.K.T model of lesson plan talks about the methods used in presenting the instructional content. In the conventional model, it is called methodology. This has been discussed extensively in the earlier part of this chapter.

Evaluation
Evaluation as pointed out earlier in this chapter means the systematic process of knowing the extent by which the instructional objectives are achieved. In the T.K.T model two types of evaluation are

identified which include students and teachers evaluation. The teacher's evaluation is a self appraisal of the teachers performance during the instructional process. Jeremiah (2013) notes that this is one of the major setbacks of the T.K.T model as it makes the teachers to be a judge in his own case.

Parts of a Lesson Plan (Constructivist Model)
Constructivist Based Instructional Models
In line with constructivist approach to learning various instructional models that are learner centred have been developed and adapted for use in the school system. Some are based on problem-based learning, while others are based on inquiry learning. Some of the constructivist based instructional models are; the five 'Es' model developed by George and Harward (1998), Guided Inquiry Supporting Multiple literacies model developed by Palincar (1998) and PEDDA-5-steps conceptual changemodel developed by Nworgu (1998). This aspect a bid to provide aconstructivist based instructional format adapts the PEDDA-5-Steps conceptual change model.

Parts of a Lesson Plan (Constructivist Model)
PEDDA-5-Steps Conceptual Change Teaching Model
The PEDDA-5-Steps conceptual change model was developed by Nworgu (1998). In this model, the process is explained using the term PEDDA to identify the step by step process involved in

presenting an instructional content. PEDDA according to Nworgu, means Prior conception, Exploration, Discussion, Dissatisfaction and Application. Agulana and Nwachukwu (2004) explained the five steps as follows:

Step I:

Identification of Prior Conception: Learners have some ideas or prior notion about natural phenomena which they bring to the science class. These views should be identified by the teacher and treated with a high degree of importance and respect no matter how illogical or infinitive they may be. They should be regarded as alternative way of looking at nature.

Step II:

Exploration of the Phenomenon: Having expressed their initial view about the phenomenon, learner are helped and organized to explore their ideas about the phenomenon. The teachers role here, should be limited to that of a facilitator, encouraging learners to gather appropriate information, execute activities and conduct experiment' Learners should be organized into smaller groups to engage in relevant activities.

Step III:

Discussion of the Findings: The learners at this stage are made to discuss results of their investigation. This could be in general session where each group would present their result and problem encountered for discussion. The discussion should be learner dominated and not teacher dominated. The teacher should only moderate the learners input. It is at this stage that the concept emerges. As the concept emerges the teacher names and explains them and then writes them on the chalkboard.

Step IV:
Dissatisfaction with Prior Conception: The teacher at this stage assists the learners to reconcile their prior conception with the conception that emerge from their activities. At this stage, learners may now feel dissatisfied or not with the pre-notion they had about the phenomenon. If learners still hold misconceptions about the phenomenon, they are made to return to stage two of the instructional sequence.

Factors that Influence Curriculum Implementation and Instruction in Nigeria
In the earlier part of this work, we have examined the concept of curriculum implementation was-examined. It was observed that curriculum implementation is one of the stages of curriculum development process. Curriculum implementation involves the classroom effort of teachers, students and other stakeholders in putting into action or operation what is obtained in the curriculum document. This implies that curriculum is implemented in the school and the major actor in such implementation process is the teacher. For effective curriculum implementation certain factors

has to be examined. These factors according to Afangideh (2009) are as follows:

Availability and utilization of Instructional Materials:
Instructional materials relative to its uses and application plays a significant role in the teaching learning process. Instructional materials in this context can be regarded as the various resources used by the teacher in the teaching learning process aimed at achieving the objectives of the lesson. Such materials may be visual, audio or audio-visual depending on the sense it appeals to. A simple analysis of the definition given above and others that may be sited by different scholars indicate the importance of instructional materials in the teaching learning process. Jeremiah (2009) explained that adequate use and application of relevant instructional materials helps to make the instructional process to be concrete rather than abstract thus enhancing students' participation, achievement and retention. For effective curriculum implementation, teacher should strive to provide relevant instructional materials that takes care of the educational needs and developmental characteristics of the learners at different levels.

❖ **Management Support:**
Effective curriculum implementation at any level also depends on management support. Management support in this regard involves the entire process of

how the educational institution is coordinated to achieve desired goal and objective. It also involves the effective allocation of human and material resources in the educational sector. Management support has some important variables such as adequate funding, provision of learning opportunities, provision of learning resources, proper dissemination of information, providing support for teachers and providing ways for teachers to network and share ideas. It also involves good leadership styles and other- motivational variables. When these variables are properly considered and channeled towards the academic achievement of the learner, curriculum implementation becomes an easier task on the part of the teacher and others concerned.

❖ **Teachers Effectiveness:**

The teacher is a significant factor in the implementation process of any school curriculum. At the stage of curriculum implementation, the teacher designs the scheme of work, unit plan, lesson plan and finally present the lesson in the class. Within the classroom, the teacher adopts adequate teaching methods, instructional materials, proper interaction pattern, classroom management and evaluation technique. These and other instructional behaviour of the teacher requires a high level of competence, which can only be demonstrated by a professional teacher.

❖ **The Learner:**

147

In contemporary educational system, the school curriculum is structured based on the felt needs and interest of the learner. This justifies the reason why in modern education literature, we have concepts such as learner centred methods, learner or child centred curriculum, child centred education and of more recent, the child friendly school approach to teaching and learning. The nature and characteristics of the learner should determine the content of the curriculum. The works of Jean Piaget explain to us the various levels of cognitive development which provide a road map for planning and implementation. Apart from these, teacher should consider themotivational variables of the learner, interest, readiness and level of individual differences. Without adequate consideration of the learner curriculum implementation may not be realised.

Factors that militate against curriculum implementation in Nigeria:
The various factors that militate or hinders effective curriculum implementation are outlined by Afangideh (2009) as follows: curriculum overload, large class population, dearth of instructional materials, teachers factor, examination malpractice, learner related issues and evaluation of learning. Others may include poor management and funding, changing continence of school curriculum, political interference and non-professionalization of teaching in Nigeria. Each of these factors are discussed relative to the Nigerian system of education.

Poor Management and Funding:
The effective functioning of any organization depends on proper funding and management. Education as a social institution need to be properly funded and managed in order to achieve set goals and objectives. In Nigeria and most part of the developing countries of the world, it can be observed that educational sector is poorly funded and managed. In many situations, budget allocation to education in Nigeria fall short of the 26% benchmark as recommended by relevant international organization. The resultant effect is poor infrastructure in terms of teaching and learning facilities, inadequate manpower and poor teaching and learning which altogether lead, to poor achievement and retention on the part of the learners. Considering the above situations, and problem implementation of school curriculum become more apparent than real. The statistics below is presented by Okoroma (2016) indicates the budgeting allocation to education from 2001 – 2016.

Table 1: Federal Budget and Educational Sector Share (2001-201 6)

Years	Total Budget	Allocation to Education	% Allocation to Education
2001	894,214,805,186	66,441,434,271	7.13
2002	578,582,851,520	63,856,955,913	6.90
2003	699,057,649,979	59,1 46,740,250	7.75
2004	889,154,844,588	60,495,410,864	5.24
2005	1,354,615,243,138	79,911,096,069	8.21
2006	1,518,877,922,467	88,150,303,003	10.43
2007	1,880,923,949,983	95,702,067 069	9.75
2008	2,213,230,236,349	97,712,819,757	10.04
2009	3,101,813,750,626	102,940,740,202	8.79
2010	3,931,265,321,767	126,729,399,627	7.37
2011	3,571,81 5,678,134	1 27,860,445,381	9.32
2012	3,945,036,061,331	136,158,572,828	9.86
2013	4,920,000,000,000	141,008,230,959	10.21
2014	6,620,000,000,000	493,400,000,000	10.68
2015	4,500,000,000,000	492,034,986,591	10.93
2016	6,080,000,000,000	369,600,000,000	8.08

Sources: Okoroma (2017)

The table shows that the Federal Government has consistently failed to implement the UNESCO agreement that at least 26% of National budgets should be allocated to education. Nigeria is a signatory to this important agreement which has been implemented in many countries that are enjoying qualitative education.

Curriculum Overload:
In recent times, this factor has constituted a major problem that has hindered effective curriculum implementation in our school system. Curriculum overload refers to the additional input on the content area or the programme offered in the school. Strictly speaking, there is nothing wrong in in the addition of new knowledge into the existing school programme. But it becomes unprofessional when such programmes are added without due consideration to the learner, the society, the teacher and even curriculum development agencies. Curriculum overload emerges as a result of innovations introduced in our educational system. Such innovator may call for or lead to the emergence of new subject area, new content, methodologies and approaches to teaching and learning. For example at the primary school level in the early 80s to 90s the school curriculum was structured around eight subject areas. Such subject areas were properly reflected in the school timetable which enhanced in-depth study as the teachers were properly trained for such subject areas. At present, the Primary or Basic Education Curriculum has witness a geometric increase in the number of subjects offered. New subjects areas such as Quantitative and Verbal Reasoning, Vocational Aptitude, Phonics, Civic Education, French, Music, Cultural and

Creative Arts. In most private schools, they even claim to offer what they call America/British Curriculum, which to them it falls within the subset of America and British education. In other situations, some schools also claim to offer the Montessori Curriculum with its attendant content area, methodology and mode of evaluation. The effect of these is that most of these subjects are not properly captured in the school timetable for effective delivery process. Even when they are captured most teachers are not properly trained in the content area and methodology of these subjects. In a situation such as these, the effective implementation of the school programme becomes a mirage.

Large Class Population:
This can also be referred to, teacher student ratio. That is the percentage of student to the teachers in a school or a particular subject. Class population has a direct effect on the instructional process i.e. curriculum implementation. Elements of curriculum implementation include classroom management or communication, uses and application of adequate teaching methods, instructional materials, teaching skills and adequate evaluation procedure. For the fact that these elements are carried out in the classroom, it therefore implies that the nature and characteristics of the classroom will pose a significant effect on these variables. In Nigeria and most of the developing countries of the world, the classroom is over populated highly above the

National Policy on Education recommendation of 1 teacher to 35 pupils. In most urban areas, a teacher teaches over 150 students clustered in deprived classrooms. In some situations, the classrooms are so dilapidated without good ventilation, roof, furniture for students and teachers, chalkboard, appliances, etc. In other situation according to Jeremiah (2004) and Gbamanja (2014) children are compelled to learn under shady trees. In situation such as these the instructional content delivery is influenced by the changing whether condition. Such situations as stated above may not enhance individualized instruction, child friendly approaches of teaching, application of appropriate teaching methods and materials and above all effective classroom management. These factors are subsets that constitute a problem to curriculum implementation. -

Dearth of Instructional Materials:
Instructional materials constitute a major component of curriculum implementation. Instructional materials in most situations are also called teaching materials, curriculum materials, apparatus, resource materials and even teaching aids. It is important to note that little difference exist between instructional materials and teaching aids when applied professionally. For the purpose of this work, instructional materials and teaching aids may be used interchangeably. Technically, instructional materials are those resources used by the teacher in the teaching learning process aimed at achieving the

objectives of the lesson. Such instructional materials may be visual, audio or audio-visual depending on the sense organ it appeals to. The importance of instructional materials in the instructional process cannot be overemphasized. It makes the learner to participate effectively in the instructional process by making learning to be concrete rather than abstract in Nigeria and most parts of the developing countries of the world. Educators and concerned citizens have observed the sorry state of instructional materials used in our school system. Science laboratories in many schools across Africa, especially West Africa are dusty rooms with little or no functional equipment. Vocational and technical subjects are taught without workshop. Government and other agencies pay lip services in the supplies of relevant instructional materials. Even when this is done, teachers are not given relevant training on how to use such materials. In this situation, delivery system and mode are still stereotyped and dogmatic and theoretical teaching seems to be the order of the day. Effective curriculum implementation becomes a mirage in a situation such as this.

Teachers Factor:
The teachers characteristics also have significant effect on curriculum implementation. A teacher is an individual who is professionally trained in art of teaching. This implies that any person who find himself in the classroom must have the needed knowledge to qualify as teacher. Closely related to this experience. Experience simply means years of

154

service. In Nigeria, and most parts of West Africa, most people that parade themselves in the classrooms are not trained teachers. They hold qualifications that are not regarded as teaching qualification. For example in Nigeria, the National Policy on Education (2004) states that the minimum qualification for teaching is the NCE. Most schools have people that fall short of such qualifications handling the chalk. Such people lack the professional ethics of teaching as such they constitute nuisance in the classroom. Closely related to this event is, when the teacher is professionally trained, such a teacher may be recruited to teach subject areas far from his specialization. In a survey conducted by Jeremiah (2004), he observes that less that 12% of teachers teaching Basic Science at the primary school level in Rivers State Nigeria specialize in Primary Science. In such situation, the teacher may lack the needed knowledge on the content area and methodology of teaching the subject. At the secondary school level, we have seen situations were - political science teachers are made to teach Physical and Health Education, Home Economics teachers teach Introductory Technology, Biology teachers teaching Government, and even Civic Education, while Physics teachers teaches Christian Religious Knowledge. These arrangements do not enhance qualitative instructional delivery aimed at facilitating curriculum implementation.

Examination Malpractice:

In Nigeria and most of the developing parts of the world, we cannot dispense the issues of the problems that militate against curriculum implementation without a good reference to examination malpractice. Examination is an instrument used by various stratas of people and authorities to measure achievement of certain predetermined objectives. The government used it to assess the extent to which the goals of the curriculum have been realized. It measures the extent to which it satisfies the needs of the society. To the management, it is used to ascertain whether or not an employee merit the next higher level in terms of promotion or employment. To the school authorities, it is used to evaluate the effectiveness of their academic programmes. In this regard the objective is to find out how equipped the students are to face the world, having passed through the course of study over a period of time in an institution of learning. To the teacher, it is used to determine the efficacy of teaching methods as it affects students achievement and retention. The extent to which examination will actualize these objectives depend on the adherence of some established standards. Thus, any act by an individual to run contrary to these set rules and regulation either before, during or after the examination constitute examination malpractice. Oniye and Alawale (2008) explain that examination malpractice is any act carried out before, during and after an examination which is against the rules set out for the proper and orderly conduct of the exam

WAEC (2004) mentioned that examination malpractice is any irregular behaviour exhibited by a candidate or anybody charged with the conduct of examination in and outside the 'examination. Examination malpractice also involves deliberate act of wrong doing, contrary to official examination rules and is designed to place a candidate at an unfair advantage or disadvantage.

The implications of examination malpractice on the school curriculum are many sided. Offorma (2006) enumerates them as follows:

- ❖ Invalid and unreliable data supplied to the system.
- ❖ Learners become lazy as many do not want to work hard since they can cheat and succeed in the examination.
- ❖ Indiscipline in school and the society in general as students do not bother about their academic work, rather time is spent planning for different evils — absenteeism, cultism, rape, theft, etc.
- ❖ Disparity in the set curriculum objectives and the attained objectives.

In a situation saddled with these after effect of examination malpractice, curriculum implementation becomes a mirage.

Learner Related Issues:

Learners are crucial factors in the implementation of a school curriculum, as such the nature and disposition of the learner must influence curriculum delivery. In our contemporary society, our young learners seem to lack interest as a result of non - adherence to social norms and value. Our value system seems to be eroded. The larger society do not value hard work and excellence in all ramification. People value quick money rather than working hard through education to make such money. The result of this is that they fail to attend classes, read their books, carryout class work and assignment. Hence on their own, the curriculum or syllabus is not covered relative to the prescribed content. A situation that leads to poor achievement, retention and attitude at all levels of education. It also encourages examination malpractice on the deliberate effort to make up for their deficiencies. Learners also fail to come to school with relevant study materials such as textbooks, work books, note books and other related materials. At the primary and secondary school levels, teachers even complain that pupils fail to come to school with pen and even correct uniform. When learners pose these negative attitudes towards learning, the task of implementing the school curriculum becomes more difficult than expected.

Evaluation of Learning:
Evaluation plays a significant role in curriculum implementation. Evaluation generally has to do with passing valid judgment about the worth of an entity.

Under instructional point of view, it involve a systematic process of knowing the extent by which instructional objectives are achieved. Curriculum implementation is carried out in the class through a structured lesson plan. Hence, it becomes clear that the nature and content of evaluation has significant influence on students performance. A good evaluation must be relevant to the specific objectives, take into consideration the developmental characteristics of the learner and above all measures, the three domains of education such as cognitive, affective and psychomotor domain. Quit often in stating objectives in lesson plans, teachers state affective objectives, but in evaluating learning outcome, not much is done to reflect the emphasized affected objectives. Teachers must be well informed to reflect the emphasized affective objectives. Teachers must be made to understand how to obtain evidence or data on affective outcomes as well as how to record the obtained evidence. Further, it does appear that teachers are yet to master the continuous assessment skills. Most teachers still emphasize on cognitive learning outcome at the expense of both the affective and psychomotor behaviour and they do continuous testing rather than continuous assessment. When instructional outcomes are not properly evaluated, it constitutes a problem to curriculum implementation.

Changing Countenance of School Curriculum:
The arbitrary changes introduced into our school curriculum if not properly evaluated can constitute

a major problem in the implementation of school curriculum. Nigeria operates a centralized curriculum model with a central curriculum development body vested with the responsibilities of designing and disseminating curriculum innovation to our schools. In view of this, the task of these curriculum development bodies remain very difficult as they are always faced with the challenges of identifying changes in societal needs and aspiration and other factors that will be infused into the school curriculum at all time. This singular factor and others have led to frequent changes in the school curriculum leading to the emergence of new subject areas out of the existing ones. For example in Nigeria, new subject areas such as citizenship education, entrepreneurship studies, foreign and local languages are introduced into the school curriculum at both primary, secondary and tertiary levels of our education. Content areas such as population and family life education, sexuality education and security studies, computer appreciation, environmental education, etc. have been infused into primary and secondary school curriculum into subject areas such as Basic Science, Social Studies, Language Arts, Integrated Science, Introductory Technology, Business Studies, History and even Religious Studies. In most situations, curriculum development in these innovative areas do not take into consideration the various steps in curriculum development process as earlier mentioned in this work. At the tertiary level, this has also reflected in general studies course where subject areas or courses are arbitrarily introduced without due consideration. Situation such as these makes our learner to be confused and lack focus on learning. Apart from these, teachers are not also properly trained to implement these infused innovations and new subject areas frequently introduced into our school system. A situation such as these hinders the implementation of school curriculum.

Political Interference

Politics has to do with the control of political power. It is who gets what, at what time and cost? Politics exist in a situation were there is inequality in social interaction. It therefore implies that politics exist at home, school, church, mosque, community, state and among nations. As a social institution, politics has constantly affected our educational system from the colonial era to the present time. During the missionary or the colonial era, educational institutions were established on political reasons. To train teachers and interpreters who will help to spread the Word of God in order to enhance the growing commercial empire of the Europeans, through colonization process. From the period of independence to the present era, political factors have constantly influence the direction of Nigerian education. The various U.P.E programme of the regional government emerged as a result of political factor. Free education was used as a political programme in spreading political ideology aimed at running election. During the second Republic (1979

- 1983) opposition states of the West that were loyal to the ideology of free education were starved of fund, making it difficult to implement the U.P.E scheme which their dominant party U.P.N advocates. In Nigeria, appointment of heads of higher institutions such as Vice Chancellor, Rector and Provost by the visitor is based on political consideration. In our universities, some times appointment of Head of Department, Directors and other Principal Officers also follows the same political consideration. Promotion to professorial position, chief lecturers are also done with high degree of political collaboration. This also applies to the various unions responsible for teachers affairs in the states such as the N.U.T. In a situation such as these competences, credibility and honesty is eroded, paving way for mediocre who may have little or no knowledge in piloting the affair of education to do so. This has placed Nigerian education in a negative limelight thus constituting a problem to curriculum implementation.

Non-Professionalization of Teaching in Nigeria
In the past decades government has taken some bold step to professionalize teaching in Nigeria. These effort include the introduction of Teachers Registration Council (T.R.C.N), Training and Retraining of Teachers and Government Policy Statement on Teacher Education as contained in the National Policy on Education. These efforts are commendable but are not adequate enough for one to say that teaching in Nigeria is a profession

compared to law, medicine, and engineering, etc. teaching in Nigeria fall short of most basic characteristics of true profession. Teaching is the only profession in Nigeria were a non teacher can be appointed minister or commissioner for education. In the political history of Nigeria, a teacher or non professional has never served as minister of Health or Justice. Closely related to this, teaching in Nigeria still suffers the problem of low public prestige. People do not have regards for teachers as such the profession tend to attract people who seem to have failed in other areas. Teaching in Nigeria also have the problem of lack of coordinated union. The various unions with the teaching profession such as ASUU, COEASU, ASUP, and NUT are so fragmented only advocating for pay raise and other welfare packages for their members. They do not struggle for the entire interest of teachers in Nigeria as obtained in other profession. Teaching in Nigeria records the least entry point as compared to other professions such as law and medicine. In Nigeria, the minimum qualification for teaching is N.C.E which is far below those of other profession. Teaching in Nigeria also suffer from the problem of non enforcement of code of conduct if any in our educational institution, teachers are found exhibiting many forms of misconduct inimical to the teaching profession. Such misconduct ranges from falsification of students result, examination malpractice, sorting, and sexual abuse. Such acts from teachers are not punished relative to the rubberstamp position of the enabling laws establishing the profession. In a

163

situation such as these, quality of instructional delivery will be positively skewed as no educational system and the entire nation can grow above the quality of its teachers.

Summary and Conclusion:
This chapter has examined among others the concept of curriculum implementation, teaching and instruction. To this view, the process of curriculum implementation which include proper analysis of the syllabus scheme of work and lesson plan, based on the conventional, T.K.T and the constructivist model were also presented with the view of a systemic analysis of their parts and areas of differences and similarities. The chapter also examined the factors that influence curriculum implementation and instruction and lastly problem of curriculum implementation in Nigeria. The chapter therefore conclude that for effective curriculum implementation, the educational system should be totally re-examined taking into consideration the various problems of curriculum implementation as discussed in this chapter, as no nation can grow above the quality of its educational system.

CHAPTER SIX

INSTRUCTIONAL METHODS

Introduction

In one of the precious chapters of this work, we examined the concept of curriculum implementation and instruction. On this basis therefore, it was noted that curriculum is implemented in the class. This probably motivated the reason why we noted that curriculum implementation is the classroom effort of teachers and students in putting into operation or action what is obtained in the curriculum document. At the stage of curriculum implementation, the major actor is the teacher who adopts different technicalities in transforming the curriculum document into action. One of the activities of the teacher at this stage is the uses and applications of appropriate teaching methods. To this effect therefore, this chapter examines among other things the concept of teaching methods, types of teaching methods relative to their advantages, set backs, mode of application and factors to consider in the choice of teaching methods.

Concept of Teaching Methods

Every human occupation be it farming, craftwork, painting and other artisans has a sort of method. The proper application of adequate methods make work easy in such human activities. Teaching as activity or a profession also has methods. It is the

165

proper application of such methods in the teaching learning process that distinguishes a professional teacher from other outside the teaching profession.

Technically speaking, there are so many definitions of teaching methods as there are authorities in education. Anyanwu (2001) notes that method is the term used to describe an established order of performing any activity or conducting any operation. Anyanwu further stated that teaching method is the overall procedure which is employed in teaching any given lesson. Methods encompass strategies, technique and skills of teaching and it include all the means and procedures which are involved in teaching to achieve educational goals.

Keziah and Ajoku (2003) in Jeremiah (2009) identify some questions which need to be followed in defining the concept of teaching method. Such questions are; what? For what? Why? and how? To them, the how of it is the method. Methodology is both the study of different methods and the systematic means of presenting subject contents and learning experiences with a view to achieving the predetermined objectives. It involves the study and practices of various teaching methods.

Jeremiah and Vipene (2013) in their study explain that teaching method is the general process or procedure used by the teacher in organizing the teaching-learning process with the sole aim of achieving the objectives of the lesson. Teaching method is a recurrent instructional technique applicable to other subjects which can be learned and applied by any teacher. This implies that teaching methods cannot be for a particular subject only or adoptable by only one teacher. It should be applicable to other subject areas by different teachers. In a nutshell, this means that every subject area has its methodology. Such methods can only be manipulated by specialist within the subject area. Teaching methods are usually named after dominant activities involved in the course of the learning process. The manifestation of such activities by the teacher and learner in one course of the adaptation is very vital. For example, in play-way, discussing or project methods of teaching are so called because of the dominant activities involved while using them in the class. In real classroom situation, Jeremiah (2009) explains that no teaching method can be used in complete isolation. Teachers in the teaching learning process utilizes combinations of methods. For example, in a physical and health education class for J.S II on the topic skills of soccer, a teacher can use demonstration method, discussion and even Socratic methods of teaching. This justifies the reason why some scholars contend that we don't have a single method of teaching but methods of teaching.

Various Teaching Methods
As earlier pointed out in this work, that teaching methods are several processes or procedures used by the teacher in organizing the teaching learning

167

process so as to achieve the objective of a particular lesson. Teaching methods according to Jeremiah (2009) can be classified into three broad groups such as Teacher-centred Methods, Learner centred Methods and Innovative Methods. The Teacher-centred Method traditional approaches of teaching that focuses more on the interest teacher rather than that of the learners. The Teacher-centred Method sees the teachers role principally as that of director of studies and work on the assumption that in all learning situation, the teachers role is superior and above all the best. The methods focus more on what is to be taught rather than the child who is taught so that the instructional process is seen more as working through the syllabus than trying to help each child develop inherent potentials. In such methods, emphasis is on teaching rather than learning. Teacher-centred Methods include, lecture, demonstration and story telling methods.

On the contrary, the Learner-centred Methods focus on the interest and active participation of the learner in the teaching-learning process. The teaching method centers on the child felt needs and interest. The methods have both psychological and philosophical undertone. On the psychological point of view, the Learner-centred Methods are based on theories of learning that throw much insight on the importance of learners involvement in activities in the teaching learning process. The philosophical considerations of these methods are progressivism and pragmatism. These two philosophical ideas stresses the importance of the learner and activities in any learning engagement. The Learner- centred Methods considered includes play-w, project discussion and filed trip methods of teaching. These methods and others are discussed relative to their advantages and disadvantages. The innovative methods emerge as a result of research works conducted on human learning and applied in the teaching learning process. These include constructivism, concept mapping, flipped teaching, cooperative method, and mobile teaching.

Lecture Method of Teaching

The lecture method of teaching is also referred to as talk and chalk method. It is a traditional method of teaching which many scholars considers outdated in meeting the demand of modern principles and practice of education. The method involves verbal presentation of ideas, facts, concept and principles. The practice in this regard is that of spoon feeding the learners with information or fact while the learners listen and take down notes. The teacher talk most of the time thus making the teaching learning process teacher-centered while the learners are merely passive who must accept the information presented by the teacher.

Advantages of Lecture Method

* ❖ The teacher focuses mainly on the instructional content. The teacher may not have much time to digress to other areas that are not important to the lesson.

❖ This method can help in the development of language skills of the learners. Such skills include listening, reading and writing skills. This is because as the lesson is going on, the learner is left with no alternative than to write down important ideas.

❖ Lecture method of teaching is most suitable for large class as characterized by most learning environment in Nigerian higher institutions

❖ The method can help in the development of independent learning. This is because after the lesson, the learner will want to read or research more to equip himself with more information. Such independent learning in many situations enhances discovery learning which is inconsistent with contemporary world of science.

❖ Lecture method can be used to cover wide area of the curriculum many topics can be treated within a short period of time. In this regard it saves the teachers time and Cost of producing instructional materials.

Disadvantages of Lecture Method

❖ The teacher spends greater time in talking as little or no instructional materials may be used during the lecture.

❖ Lecture method is didactic. The learner is easily frustrated and may manifest some negative characteristic that will be inimical to the achievement of the lessons objective.

170

- The learner under the lecture method of teaching is passive thus he cannot develop good sense of inquiry and creativity.
- Learning through active involvement is completely omitted. This is because the learner is placed in the position of listener.
- The method is textbook dominated. This encourages rote learning and the regurgitation of information without necessarily aiding understanding.
- The lecture method of teaching is limited for use at the higher levels of education as such it may not be universally applied at, lower levels of education mostly the pre-primary and primary school level.

Ways of Improving on the use of Lecture Method

- The teacher can ask questions which involve critical thinking at various segment of the lesson.
- The teacher should adopt effective communication skill, use appropriate language relative to the developmental characteristics of the learner.
- Teacher should maintain constant interaction or dialogue with the learners in order to minimize boredom on the part of the learner. This can be achieved through questions and also motivating pupils to learn.
- Lecture method should be used specifically to develop concept directed to principles and generalization. Science teachers should try to

minimize the use of lecture method in presenting scientific concepts. Facts are easily forgotten when presented verbally.

❖ Lecture method by itself should not be used in isolation in any one lesson. If you use it to introduce a lesson, strive to use another method to develop the lesson. This implies that lecture method should be supplemented with other methods.

Demonstration Method

This method involves teaching and displaying of something i.e. an audiovisual explanation of an idea, process and product involves doing and telling learners the point of emphasis. This method enhances development of manipulative skills using various senses. For example, a teacher needs to demonstrate the dissection of toad or rabbit in Biology class or distillation process in Chemistry class. Other subjects that make effective us of demonstration method include Home Economics, Physical Education, Introductory Technology and Agricultural Science.

Advantages of Demonstration Method

❖ The method enhances proper classroom management because the classroom remain orderly as the teacher handles and demonstrates with the apparatus.

❖ The method can be used to develop learners interest since it involves the use of audio-visual materials and other related facilities.

172

- ❖ The method - is economical in terms of money and time. The teacher spends few times in explanation, also few equipments may be needed by the to carry out his demonstration activities.
- ❖ Demonstration method can be used to develop observational skill or competences of the learner.
- ❖ Demonstration method can be used to introduce a lesson or it can also be used to end a lesson.

Disadvantages of Demonstration Method
- ❖ Demonstration may be dominated by the teacher making the lesson teacher centered.
- ❖ The method does not give pupils any opportunity to discover things or to solve problems on their own.
- ❖ If a demonstration fails, students may loose confidence on the teacher. This can induce negative attitude towards the subject.
- ❖ Visibility may sometimes be poor in this regard, learners may have difficulty in seeing details of object being demonstrated.

Ways of Improving on the use of Demonstration Method
- ❖ Teachers should ensure proper mastery of demonstrated items or skills before presenting it to the class.
- ❖ Teachers should make demonstration visible to all the learners in the class.

❖ This can be carried out through grouping the learners into smaller groups. Teachers should constantly check on the learners understanding. Teachers should not let the learners be bored or frustrated due to their lack of understanding.

❖ Teachers should ensure successful demonstration always as failure may lead to pupils losing confidence on the teacher.

Story Telling Method of Teaching

Story telling method of teaching involves the use of related story in explaining an instructional content. Some scholars in the field of education are of the opinion that this method is limited to certain subjects are such as History, Literature, Religious Knowledge, Social Studies and other art subjects. This is not true, the story telling method, if properly applied by a skillful teacher can be used in teaching variety of subjects in both arts and science. For example, Jeremiah and Job (2011) confirm that story telling is an important tool for set induction in presenting an instructional content.

Advantages of Story Telling Method

❖ This method can be used in the development of speaking skill on the part of the learner. Speaking skill is one of the expressive skills of language.

❖ The method enhances the learner to learn the rudiment of grammar.

174

- ❖ Facts and figures can be presented when story telling method is properly adopted.
- ❖ The method is based on the philosophy that children love story and that the best way to teach them is through story.
- ❖ It helps in the arrangement and organization of event in the story.

Disadvantages of Story Telling Method
- ❖ Sometimes the story may not be a true reflection of the event. This may lead to confusion on the part of the learners.
- ❖ The use of story telling makes the teacher to dominate the lesson therefore making the teaching learning process teacher centered rather than learner centered.
- ❖ Some stories may be too long that the teacher may not have the time to explain the main ideas of the lesson.
- ❖ The method can only be executed by a skillful teacher.

Ways of Improving on the use of Story Telling Method
- ❖ Teachers should avoid telling stories that do not teach morals.
- ❖ Teachers should avoid telling complicated stories involving too many characters.
- ❖ Avoid telling stories that will frighten the learner.
- ❖ Tell stories that are within the comprehension level of the learners.

Play-Way Method of Teaching

The play-way method of teaching was propounded by Froebel and was made popular by Maria Montessori. It is a method of teaching in which the instructional content is presented to the learner in a playful fashion and the learner is made to learn the concept unconsciously. Play-way method of teaching is anchored on the philosophy that children by nature love play. Since they love play, the best approach of teaching them should be through the use of play. The play-way method of teaching is more prominent for use at the pre-primary school level relative to their developmental characteristics. It may not be popular for use at the senior primary and secondary school levels of education.

Advantages of Play-Way Method of Teaching

- ❖ The method allows group and individual participation as the learners are made to play with each group individually.
- ❖ Children learn the rules and regulations guiding the play. This can enhance co-existence, and tolerance among the learners right from this early stage.
- ❖ The play-way method of teaching enhances active participation of learners in the instructional process. Such participation can call forbetter achievement, retention and the development of positive attitude towards the instructional process.

❖ Play-way method takes into consideration the level of individual differences of the learner. Hence the method is learner friendly.
❖ Play is a recreation, it recreate both body and mind. Such, enhances the development of effective characteristics of the learner.

Disadvantages of Play-Way Method
❖ The play-way method of teaching can only be executed by a skillful teacher. Such skills can be acquired through training such as seminars, workshop, conferences, etc.
❖ Cultural background of the teacher may pose some challenges on the use of play-way method. This problem can be solved through proper pre-service and in-service programmes for the teacher. Adequate recruitment procedure can also help to minimize the effect of this problem.
❖ The play-way method of teaching is expensive. It involves many materials, facilities and other teaching aids for its implementation. In terms of manpower, it also need special training on the part of the teacher.
❖ In many situations, the play-way method is limited to the preprimary and primary school levels. This implies that its application is limited.
❖ Play may offend some learners mostly when such play is against their views, and emotional disposition.

- ❖ Introverts in the class may not benefit by the use of play-way method. Such group of learners may shy away from the play.

Project Method of Teaching:
The project method of teaching can be classified as a form of individualized instruction that involves the learner performing a task or activities in a natural manner and in a spirit of purpose to accomplish a difficult goal. The project in a learning unit is usually conducted by individual student or some times by group of students under the guidance of the teacher. The project topic is chosen based on the background experience of the student and the work to be accomplished is to be an original work of the student or student performing task. Sources of project work may include academic journal, learners experience, topic based on field work, socio-economic problems, creative work in arts, such as music, poetry, drawing and painting. Project could be conducted on short term or long term basis depending on the nature of the topic, availability of time and other environmental factors. Gbamanja (2001) explains that project should be undertaken because:
- ❖ The topic is interesting
- ❖ The learner can pursue the task and accomplish his own solution.
- ❖ They will provide means of inculcating the scientific method on the learner.
- ❖ They offer opportunities for exhibiting ingenuity.

178

Characteristics of Genuine Project

The following are some major characteristics of genuine project as noted by Gbamaja (2001).

❖ The investigator (learner) must have genuine interest on the project at hand. It should not be a drudge but should be performed somewhat like hobby or leisurely pursuit.

❖ There should be a primary aim to earn something from the findings or results of the project.

❖ The investigator must exhibit original work in terms of procedures in arriving at the solution of the problem.

❖ Cost should be minimal. Use of inexpensive local materials and improvisation skills must be maintained.

❖ The scientific method of solving problems must be encouraged.

Advantages of Project Methods

❖ It motivates the learner mostly when he is able to perform a task and arrive at a worthwhile answer to the problem.

❖ It facilitates individual learning. This help in the development of self-confidence in the learner.

❖ Project method helps in the development of the spirit of creativity, originality and freedom of expression of the learner.

❖ The learning process is more pragmatic and result oriented through the use of project method.

* Project method is an excellent means of fostering co-operation among learners and encouraging the development of leadership qualities.

Disadvantages of Project Method
* In some situations, it is difficult to formulate project topic or idea.
* It is very tasking on the part of the teacher to adequately supervise the project to a reasonable conclusion.
* When a project work is not properly guided, its objectives may be defeated.
* Project may be expensive. Lack of equipment and resource could militate against the successful conclusion of the project.
* It may be time consuming, exceeding the learning duration stipulated in the school timetable.
* Order and discipline may be difficult to maintain on the part of the students. The students may be carried away.

Ways of Improving on the use of Project Method
* The project should not be haphazardly planned. Teacher should do proper planning, taking into consideration available time, resources and general capacity of the learners.
* Group should be well formed. Grouping could be mixed, ability or gender. Appoint a leader for such group.

- ❖ Project topic should be well chosen to fully engage students lasting interest, awaken curiosity and create a demand for new information. It must be worthwhile and educative.
- ❖ Each group should be assisted by defined instruction, encouragement and guidance as the need arises to keep them fully occupied and in the right direction.
- ❖ Reference books and other working materials should be made available at the disposal of students.
- ❖ Outside visit should be prepared in advance if deemed useful.
- ❖ Outside resource persons should be brought in, to give students talks on the topic at hand.

Discussion Method of Teaching

Discussion involves a situation whereby two or more people interact verbally with each other. Under instructional point of view, discussion method involves a situation where learners are made to pool ideas together and reach a conclusion. According to Gbamanja (2001), discussion method could be adopted deliberately in a learning situation, but sometimes it occurs spontaneously as a teacher uses one method of teaching or the other. It may be considered as a technique within a method. Sometimes it may occur at brief intervals during an informal lecture, or to be involved and so maximum participation is achieved.

Based on this perspectives, discussion could be considered as student centered method of teaching.

Jeremiah (2004) explained that in discussion method, learners and teachers consider a problem, analyze, interpret and weigh issues together before arriving at a conclusion. The method according to Jeremiah involves self-confidence and tolerance in the learners because learners must be confident enough to allow others make meaningful contributions. In discussion method, students are allowed or led to create and experience ideas rather than sit passively and receive ideas formulated and dished out by the teacher. Jeremiah (2009) further classified four approaches of discussion such as; whole class discussion, small group discussion, panel discussion and debate.

Whole Class Discussion:
This technique involves the entire class participating on the topic discussion. That is every member of the class is given the opportunity to contribute their ideas to the topic been discussed while the teacher acts as moderator. The teacher in this case directs the discussion and sharpens the focus or attention of the learners, while the students are encouraged to make comments that correspond to issues revised by themselves or by the teacher. The teacher assumes the duty of making sure that all the activities are directed towards the attainment of the desired objective and finally concludes the discussion by pooling the important points raised by the participating students. Whole class approach of discussion is important because it gives every

student equal opportunity to contribute his or her ideas on the topic of discussion.

Small/Group Discussion:
This approach is more suitable for experienced students. In this situation, the teacher uses some criteria such as ability, gender, mix, interest and friendship to split the class into small group. A leader or team captain is appointed for each group. The teachers role in this type of discussion is to go round the various groups to ascertain whether the students are actually participating in the discussion. In this situation, he may direct or refocus their discussion where there is little digression from the topic by asking them questions or making comments. At the end of the discussion, each of the group leader summaries the important points to the whole class which may lead to subsequent class discussion.

Panel Discussion
In this type of discussion, the teacher may set up a panel of discussant depending on the number he wants to discuss the issue. The discussants are given the opportunity to express their ideas on the various aspect of the topic. After making one or more corrections or observations, the teacher now throw the discussion open to the whole class for more contribution. The teacher together with the class draws the main points together.

Debate:

In debate, a competitive class environment is set among contestants to debate or argue on a particular issue. Such issues are always drawn from societal problems or ideas. Speakers are selected to speak for each group, based on the agreed topic. Such speakers are assessed based on certain variables. At the end of the contribution from eachspeaker, the topic will be declared open to the floor or audience for willing members of the class to contribute their ideas.

Advantages of Discussion Method of Teaching
- ❖ It encourages participation and involvement in what is going on in the learning environment. In this regard, students acquire a variety of knowledge.
- ❖ It enables the students to develop a sense of confidence through participation and exchange of ideas.
- ❖ It develops positive interpersonal relationship because the students interact with the teacher and their colleagues on the basis of their desire to gain knowledge from one another.
- ❖ It develops critical and evaluative thinking and listening.
- ❖ The method helps students to develop language skills such as speaking, listening and reading.

Disadvantages of Discussion Method of Teaching
- ❖ The method may consume a lot of time mostly when students gives various answers which

may not be relevant to the specific objectives of the lesson.

❖ In an over populated class, it is very difficult to achieve maximum interaction.

❖ The discussion process may be dominated by extroverts or the brighter students in the class.

❖ Students who lack the knowledge or background on the topic being discussed may be disinterested in the lesson because they are not involved.

❖ Factors such as gender, age and other related variables may affect the topic of discussion.

Field Trip Method of Teaching

Field trip as a method of teaching include excursions carried out in and outside the school environment to enable learners observe a phenomenon, process or event, interact with some personalities in order to obtain some information relevant to a particular subject area, or school experience. In this regard therefore, field trip provides an important component of the learning process. It includes visit to various places, or some exciting place or important landmark. Field trip if well planned is meant to broaden students general knowledge, students will observe the application of certain concept learnt in the class. Places where teachers can utilize for field trip are banks, market, parks, hotels, media houses, rehabilitation centres, hospitals, lakes, museum, cultural centres, dams, etc. If excursions are well planned and hitch free, it broadens the students general knowledge as it affords them a wonderful experience which ordinarily would have been difficult to conceive. It stimulates students interest in the subject and the method can be used to teach any group of learners irrespective of their age and other related characteristics. Izuagba, Afurobi and Jermeiah (2014) identify various types of field trip as:

- Walking trip around a familiar room.
- A walking trip around a neighborhood
- Taking a small group of children at a time on a mini-field trip and
major field trips. They also recommended and appropriate site for
visit as:
- Be safe for visit
- Be fairly close by so that children can walk or take a car
- Not too fatiguing for the children
- Not be too crowded or noisy
- Offer the students sensory experiences
- Offer genuine learning experience through participation

Guidelines for Successful Field Trip
The following guidelines should be allowed by the teacher in organizing a successful field trip. Such guidelines are as follows:

- ❖ Visit the field trip site or location yourself and get relevant information.
- ❖ Talk to the contact person who will be there on the day you and the
children will visit and call her for verification the day before the field trip.
- ❖ Explain how many students will be involved in the visit, age of the students, class, time of visit etc should also be made known.
- ❖ Explain to the students the need to explore, see and touch where necessary during the visit.
- ❖ Find out the site rules and regulations.
- ❖ Find out the accommodation for the students if need be.
- ❖ Determine arrangement for lunch or snacks.

Jeremiah (2009) in his work prescrib the following preliminary measures to be taken in conducting a successful field trip as:
- ❖ The teacher should make preliminary contact and final arrangement with the place of visit.
- ❖ Teacher should make arrangement with the head teachers or principal about details of the trip.
- ❖ Make arrangement with other teachers so that the trip will not conflict with their class.
- ❖ Prepare a preliminary list of questions or other materials which can be helpful in planning with the students.
- ❖ Discuss the trip with the students mostly the objectives of the trip, safety, and behavioural

standards for the trip, things to look out for and information to get.

❖ Get written permission from the parents.

❖ Make good logistic arrangement in terms of transport, medical care, accommodation and feeding.

Advantages of Field Trip Method of Teaching

❖ Field trip provides primary experience to the learners.

❖ It provides a sound and concrete basis for conceptual schemes of learning.

❖ The method crystallizes learning experience and facilitates retention and transfer of knowledge.

❖ Teacher student relationship is developed more intimately.

❖ It serves as better subtitle for the use of instructional materials in the class.

Disadvantages of Field Trip Method of Teaching

❖ The method is time consuming because it takes time to plan a trip.

❖ The method is expensive in-terms of money. Money may be needed for transportation, first aid materials and other related materials that may be needed for the trip.

❖ The danger of accident during the trip may not be completely ruled out.

❖ Field trip can also disrupt other school activities.

Discovery / Inquiry Method of Teaching

In contemporary time, discovery and inquiry methods of teaching have been emphasized as potent instructional methods that can be used to enhance students achievement. Many educators apply the concept discovery or inquiry interchangeably while others may prefer to create a difference in terms of their application. In this work, we may use the two concepts differently for a proper understanding. Discovery is defined by various scholars such as Pruner (1961), Witrock (1977) and Cronbach (1966). Gbamanja (1991) citing Sword and Trowbridge (1973) explain that discovery occurs when an individual is involved mainly in using their mental processes to mediate (discover) some concepts or principles. This implies that as a result of some mental and physical activities, an individual is able to grasp concept and principles of various phenomena. Many educators who advocate for this method believe that many concept and principles in various disciples mostly in sciences should not be taught to learners, but that the learners should be left to discover the concept and principle through problem solving activities. According to Gbamanja (1991), discovery method involves an unstructured exploration in some problem solving experiences in which the student can draws general conclusion from data which he has gathered through various mental and physical process such as observing, measuring, classifying, inferring, predicting, communicating, describing and formulating relevant questions. In this process, concept and principles are formed. Thus a proper understanding of concepts leads to the formulation of relevant principles and generalization which is very vital in problem solving situation.

In emphasizing the relevance of discovery method in the teaching learning process,, Bruner noted that learning is a process, not a product. He stated further that to instruct someone in a discipline is not a matter of getting him to commit result to mind, rather, it is to teach him to participate in the process that makes possible the establishment of knowledge. Inquiry method on the contrary is anchored on discovery as both methods seem to be tied up with each other. Inquiry is carried out with a view to finding some answers or reasons why a certain problem exists. This indicates that inquiry investigation goes much further than discovery as such the learner has to utilize all his discovery capabilities in order to succeed in true inquiry. Inquiry as a problem solving technique can be traced to the work of John Deway (1933) who opines that the development of intellectual and sensitivity should be a key regard for all learners in solving problems. True inquiry involves the unraveling of the hidden relationship of nature. In order to conduct an inquiry successfully, the learner must exhibit certain relatively sophisticated mental process which are outlined by Gbamanja (2001) as follows:

❖ Asking insightful questions about natural phenomena.

- ❖ Formulating problems
- ❖ Formulating hypothesis
- ❖ Disposing investigative approaches
- ❖ Carrying out experiment
- ❖ Synthesizing knowledge
- ❖ Having certain scientific attitude as objectivity, curiosity, open- mindedness and responsibility.

In an inquiry exercise, the investigator originates his own problem, he designs his own experiment or procedure for collecting data or relevant information and he arrives at his own conclusion and subsequent principles involved. This is to say that learners can only develop discovery and inquiry abilities only if he is involved in activities requiring the performance of the mental task enumerated above. The three main types of inquiry as identified by educators are as follows:

- ❖ **Guided Inquiry**:
  This could be either inductive or deductive in nature. In the deductive model, the general principle is given and the student is required to use the principles in order to discover the solution to a specific problem. But if the solution to a problem is given and the student is required to discover the general principle on which the solution is based, the guided inquiry is adopted through the inductive process. The major issue about guided inquiry method is that it originates the problems to be solved. In order to give further guidance, the teacher may even explain, give

clues or procedures in solving the problems. The learners are closely guided towards the solution of the problem. In more simple terms, activities surrounding guided inquiry are structured by the teacher.

❖ **Free Inquiry**:
   A true free inquiry occurs when students originate and Carry out their own investigation. In this task, neither the general principle nor the solution is given and the students are required to discover both the principles and the solution. The students formulate their own problems, devise methods or procedure to solve the problems, collect their own data and draw reasonable conclusion by themselves.

❖ **Modified Free Inquiry:**
This model has a little teacher guidance as in general inquiry. In modified free inquiry, the teacher provides the problem and then the students are asked to solve the problems in their own way. In this regard, the teacher acts as a resource person only in terms of providing information or motivation but not providing clues to the solution to the problem. The teacher may ask relevant questions that may provide hints for the students but these questions should not be directed towards providing answers to the problem.

Advantages of Discovery and Inquiry Method of Teaching

Discovery and inquiry methods of teaching makes learning more student centered rather than teacher centered.

- ❖ Manipulative skills can be developed on the part of the learners as they are exposed to activities involving the use of materials and apparatus.
- ❖ This method can inculcate on the learners the spirit of self- confidence as the students are involved in the task at hand, he uses his initiative and potential in arriving at answer to problem , he realizes the self. The ago is fully identified as the learner develops a positive self-confidence
- ❖ Understanding of concepts and principles is better facilitated instead of learning by rote, and retention rate is high.
- ❖ With repeated success achieved through his own efforts, the student can always expect to succeed in any endeavour. This can enhance positive attitude to work and learning.
- ❖ Discovery and inquiry can enhance the development of talents. As the learner is given freedom to investigate a given task, he has the tendency to use various talents appropriate for the task. Talents such as creativity, social organization, communication, etc are developed.

Disadvantages of Discovery and Inquiry Method of Teaching

- ❖ The method is slow and time consuming both on the part of the learners and the teacher.
- ❖ The method is very expensive in terms of funding, considering that it requires a lot of materials and equipment
- ❖ The use of inquiry and discovery method of teaching is limited. It may be difficult to apply it in a large class, particularly, when a large amount of material and other facilities are needed.
- ❖ Students may be frustrated in the process, mostly, when they cannot provide appropriate clues to solve problems or if they cannot solve them at all.
- ❖ There is a little or no attention paid to the acquisition of recognized body of knowledge, or instruction and as such, the method appears to be contrary to the content area of the syllabus

Constructivist Instructional Method

The constructivist approach to teaching and learning according to Huit (2003) is based on a combination of a subset of research within cognitive psychology and social psychology, just as behavior modification technique are based on operant conditioning theory within behavioural psychology. The basic premise of constructivism according to Brunner (1990) is that the individual learner must actively "build" knowledge and skill and that information exist within these built construct rather than in the external environment. Jeremiah (2010) notes that all advocates of constructivism agree that it is the individual processing stimuli from the environment and the resulting cognitive structure, which produces adaptive behaviour rather than the stimuli themselves.

Andrew (2001) observes that constructivism is a view of learning based on the belief that knowledge is not a thing that can be simply given by the teacher at the front of the classroom to students on their desk. Rather knowledge is a continuous process of development; learners become the builder and creator of meaning and knowledge. Constructivism can also be observed as a philosophy founded on the premise that by reflecting on our experience we construct our own understanding of the world we live in. Each of us generates our own "role" and "mental model" which we use to make sense of our experience. Learning therefore is simply the process of adjusting our mental model to accommodate new experience. This implies that learners construct their own understanding and knowledge of the world- through experiencing things and reflecting on those experiences. When we encounter something new, we have to reconcile it with our previous ideas and experience, may be, changing what we believe or discarding the new information as irrelevant. Constructivism believe that what the learner learns is as a result of reconstruction of their previous experience.

Advantages of Constructivism

- ❖ Children learn better and enjoy learning more when they are actively involved, rather than passive listeners.

- ❖ Education work best when it focuses more on thinking and understanding rather than on rote and memorization of fact. Constructivism lay emphasis on learning how to think and understand.

- ❖ Constructivism learning is transferable. In constructivism classroom, learners create organizing principle that they can take with them to other learning setting. The implication to this is that constructivism can enhance positive transfer of learning.

- ❖ Constructivism gives students ownership of what they learn, since learning is based on students question and exploration, and often the students have a hand in designing the assessment as well. It engage the students initiative and personal investment. Engaging the creative instinct develops students abilities to express knowledge through variety & ways. On this basis therefore, students are more likely to retain and transfer the new knowledge to real life.

- ❖ By grounding learning activities in an authentic and real-world, constructivism stimulates and engages students. Students in constructivism classroom learn to question

196

things and apply their natural curiosity to the world.

❖ Constructivism promotes social and communication skills by creating a classroom environment that emphasizes collaboration and exchange of ideas.

Disadvantages of Constructivism

❖ Constructivism can only function in a situation where basic elements that promote learning are provided.

❖ Constructivism is a new theory of learning and pedagogy. As a new theory, teachers are not properly trained in its application and use in the classroom.

❖ Sometimes, the dialogue and probing between teachers and students as obtained in constructivist method may consume a lot of time. This may make the learners loose interest on what they are learning.

❖ The various constructivist model propounded by different scholars may not be generally applied in all situation. They are designed specifically to suit a given situation.

❖ Constructivist strategy can only function with children from outstanding good home background. To children from deprived home background it will be difficult to apply.

Concept Mapping Teaching Method

A concept map is a visual learning and thinking tool used to organize and structure knowledge. Concept maps were developed in 1972 through the work of

Novak which anchored on the research work developed by Ausubel (1963). In his famous work, Ausubel developed the concept of Advanced Organizer which states that learning takes through the process of assimilation of new concepts and proposition into existing concept and propositional framework held in the scheme by the learner. Ausubel postulates prior knowledge in learning new concept by stating that the most important single factor influencing learning is what the learner already knew and further advices that teachers should ascertain this and build new knowledge on it. To Novak, meaningful learning involves the assimilation of new concepts and proposition into existing cognitive structure (scheme).

Concept mapping is a good strategy for introducing or concluding a lesson and have their origin in the learning movement called Constructivism. As earlier noted in this work, the constructivist hold that prior knowledge is used as a framework to learn new knowledge. In essence, how we think influences what we learn. Concept maps identify the way we think, the way we see relationships between knowledge. This is why concept maps are as graphical thinking tool for organizing and representing knowledge. When it is developed by a working group and shared by all students, it gives a vivid picture / illustration of their reflective thought and it can become excellent process of building knowledge in a social environment that is collaborative and constructive. To put it briefly, concept map are excellent tool for a collaborative activity that will lead to a very meaningful learning as indicated in the work of Jera (2012).

In drawing a concept map, the main idea is usually enclosed in squire boxes and relationship between concepts indicated by connecting lines linking two concepts in a hierarchical order; linking words or phrases that specify the relationship between the two concepts and are written along the lines. It clarifies and visually illustrates relationship between the concept and related ones. A concept map typically represents ideas, words and information as boxes or circle. The main ideas are enclosed in boxes while related ones are enclosed in a circle which it connects with arrows in a hierarchical structure. The relationship between concept may indicate synonyms or antonyms relationships, causes and effects, main ideas and supporting ideas, chronological order etc.

Concept maps are used to develop the logical thinking, creative and critical thinking and study skills in students. It also help students see how individual ideas connects to form larger whole. One of the characteristics of concept maps is that the concept, are represented in a hierarchical order with the most general concepts (main idea) at the top of the map and the more specific less general concepts (supporting ideas) arranged hierarchically below. Another important feature of concept map is the inclusion of cross links. These are links between concepts in different domains of the concept map. The cross-links help us see how a concept in one domain of knowledge represented on the map is related to a concept in another domain shown on the map.

Novak (1990) explained that one of the reasons why concept mapping is a powerful instrument in facilitating comprehension and meaningful learning is that it serves as a kind of scaffold that helps the learner organizes knowledge and structure it which encourage top — bottom processing of information. Many learners and teachers are surprised to see how this simple tool facilitates meaningful learning and create powerful knowledge frameworks of the knowledge for long period of time. Apart from serving as a powerful thinking and learning tool, concept maps are also an evaluating tool. It can be used in identifying both valid and invalid ideas hold by students as well as identifying the relevant knowledge a learner possess before the lesson (advanced organizer) or after the lesson.

Concept Map on Marriage Institution

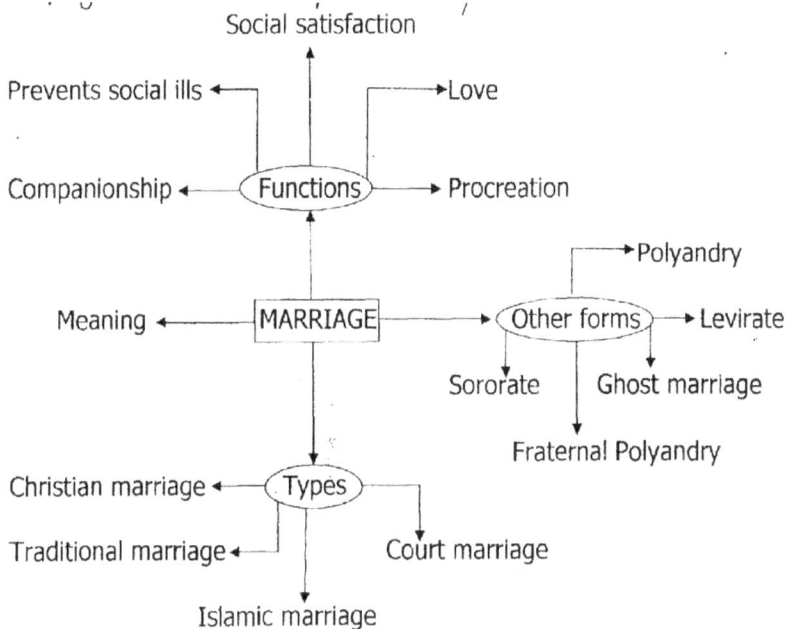

Fig. 4 **Concept Map on Marriage Institution**

Basic Characteristics of Concept Map
Izeagba, Aforobi and Jeremiah (2014) identified some basic characteristics of concept mapping as follows:
- ❖ Concept maps are formal and generally have well defined structure and less pictorial in nature.
- ❖ It is commonly use to organize and represent tacit knowledge.
- ❖ Usually contain general concept at the top of the map, with more specific concepts below arranged in a hierarchical order.

201

- ❖ Connector line usually contains key words or phrases that indicate the relationship between the topics they connect.
- ❖ Topics may be cross-linked with each other to depict more complex relationship between topics or concepts.
- ❖ It uses hierarchical structures and relational phrases to facilitate understanding of relationships and links between concepts.
- ❖ The aim of concept mapping ss not to generate spontaneous associative elements but to outline relationship between ideas. Thus concept mapping is a relational device.
- ❖ Concept map has a hierarchical "true" structure with super-ordinate and subordinate parts (primary, secondary and tertiary ideas).
- ❖ Concept map normally begins with a word or concept or phrase which forms the focus of the task.

Advantages of Concept Mapping
The advantages of concept map are s follows:
- ❖ Facilitates the transfer of export knowledge.
- ❖ Facilitate collaborative knowledge modeling.
- ❖ Facilitate the collation of shared vision and shared understanding within a team or organization.
- ❖ It is an instructional design that provides an initial conceptual form for subsequent information and learning and is adapted from advanced Organizers.

- ❖ Enhances metacognition (Learning to learn and thinking about knowledge).
- ❖ Improves language ability.
- ❖ Assesses learners understanding of learning objectives, concepts and the relationships among these concepts.

Flipped Teaching Method:
The flipped classroom is a reversal of the traditional teaching method, It is a teaching strategy where learners gain first exposure to a lesson outside the classroom usually via reading or videos or by carrying out their own research on the topic and then class time is used to do more difficult tasks on the topic which include problem solving activities, debates etc.

The key purpose of the flipped classroom is to engage students in active learning where there is a greater focus on students' application of conceptual knowledge rather than factual recall. The concept of students viewing lectures at home and tackling homework together in class, is a powerful movement in 21st century education.

The flipped classroom intentionally shifts instruction to a learner-centered model in which class time explores topics in greater depth and creates meaningful learning opportunities, while educational technologies such as online videos are used to deliver content outside of the classroom. In a flipped classroom, content delivery may take a variety of forms. Often, video lessons prepared by the teacher or third parties are used to deliver content, although online collaborative discussions, digital research, and text readings may be use

History and development of the flipped classroom

In 1993, Alison King published Qrom Sage on the Stage to Guide on the Side." In the article, King focuses on the importance of the use of class time for the construction of meaning rather than information transmission. While not directly illustrating the concept of "flipping" a classroom, King's work is often cited as an impetus for an inversion to allow for the educational space for active learning. Harvard Professor Eric Mazur played a significant role in the development of concepts influencing flipped teaching through the development of an instructional strategy he called peer instruction. Mazur published a book in 1997 outlining the strategy, entitled Peer Instruction: A User's Manual. He found that his approach, which moved information transfer out of the classroom and information assimilation into the classroom, allowed him to coach students in their learning instead of lecture.

Lage, Platt and Treglia published a paper entitled "Inverting the Classroom: A Gateway to Creating an Inclusive Learning Environment" (2000), which discusses their research on flipped classrooms at the college level. In their research focusing on two college economics courses, Lage, Platt, and Treglia assert that one can leverage the class time that becomes available from the inversion of the classroom (moving information presentation via lecture out of the classroom through media such as computers or VCRs) to meet the needs of students with a wide variety of learning styles. The University of Wisconsin-Madison deployed software to replace lectures in large lecture-based computer science course with streaming video of the lecturer and coordinated slides.

Perhaps the most recognizable contributor to the flipped classroom is Salman Khan. In 2004, Khan began recording videos at the request of a younger cousin he was tutoring because she felt that recorded lessons would let her skip segments she had mastered and replay parts that were troubling her. Salman Khan founded Khan Academy based on this model. For some, Khan Academy has become synonymous with the flipped classroom, however, these videos are only one form of the flipped classroom strategy.

The Wisconsin Collaboratory for Enhanced Learning has built two centers to focus on flipped and blended learning. The classroom structure houses technology and collaboration-friendly learning spaces, and emphasis for those involved in the program is placed on individualized learning through non-traditional teaching strategies such as flipped classroom.

Woodland Park High School chemistry teachers Jonathan Bergmann and Aaron Sams became driving forces in flipped teaching at the high school level when, in 2007, they recorded their lectures and posted them online in order to accommodate students who spent guiding knowledge and providing feedback rather than delivering direct instruction. Bergman and Sams (2012) reasoned that direct instruction could be delivered by recording video content for students to engage with before class (and any time) freeing up class time for activities that allow deeper exploration of content.

Advantages of a flipped classroom
More one-to-one time between teacher and student
A flipped classroom dramatically increases the amount of time you have to spend with each student. It also create a platform for them to ask questions or seek extra help with an area they're finding challenging.

More collaboration time for students
The project-based work that now takes place in the classroom need not be on an individual basis. A flipped classroom enables students to spend more time collaborating with one another: not only a great way to learn, but also good for their team working skills.

Students learn at their own pace

Since knowledge acquisition takes place outside the classroom, each student can control it to match their own personal abilities and aptitude. A traditional classroom instruction-based method relies on every student absorbing and understanding at the same time and pace. Flipped learning doesn't. This can be particularly liberating for slower learners. No longer do they feel the burden of having to 'keep up'; they're free to learn in a way that works for them. And if they want to go back and study something again, they can.

It encourages students to come to class prepared
After students have engaged with digital content at home, they can come to the classroom prepared with ideas and questions. It's a great way to involve students in shaping the classroom sessions, and thereby nurture their sense of responsibility.

Absenteeism
Like missing class due to illness — become less problematic. It used to be that, if a student missed a lesson, they missed learning something. Not with flipped learning. Because students engage with a lesson on their own time, and away from school, absence need not detract from them learning the material.

Subject matter content becomes infinitely richer
Previously, students were only exposed to one source of information on a topic: that which the

teacher gave them in class. With flipped learning, they can explore much more. They can access multiple sources, and equally you can direct them towards sources from other teachers, and more. This diversity will only increase their comprehension of the subject.

It is cost-effective

Because students use their own devices to access content, there's no need for a school to invest in hundreds of new computers or classroom gadgets. The only thing the teachers need to give is more of their personal time and attention.

Disadvantages of the flipped classroom

Digital divide

A central problem of the flipped classroom is how to get technology into the hands of every student. This gives room for a 'digital divide' because not all families are from the same socio-economic background, and thus access to computers or video-viewing technology outside of the school environment is not possible for all students. This model of instruction may put undue pressure on some families as they attempt to gain access to videos outside of school hours.

Lack of Self directedness in all students

Additionally, some students may struggle due to their developing personal responsibility. Students who are not at the developmental stage required to keep on track with independent learning may fall rapidly behind their peers.

Increased computer time
Flipped classroom leads to increased computer time in an era where adolescents already spend too much time in front of computer screens Inverted models that rely on computerized videos do contribute to this challenge, particularly if videos are long.

Learning Style Bias
Flipped classrooms that rely on videos to deliver instruction suffer some of the same challenges as traditional classrooms. Students may not learn optimally by listening to a lecture, and watching instructional videos at home is still representative of a more traditional form of teaching. Kinaesthetic learners do not gain much from these video lessons.

Increased Preparation Time
Increased preparation time is initially likely needed, as creating high quality videos requires teachers to contribute significant time and effort outside of regular teaching responsibilities.

Cost Burden
Additional funding may also be required to procure training for teachers to navigate computer technologies involved in the successful implementation the flipped classroom model.

Co-Operative Teaching Method.

Cooperative learning is a teaching strategy in which small teams, each with students of different ability levels, use a variety of learning activities to improve their understanding of a subject. Each member of a team is responsible, not only for learning what is taught, but also for helping their teammates learn, thus creating an atmosphere of achievement.

In order to create an environment in which cooperative learning can take place, three things are necessary. First, students need to feel safe, but also challenged. Second, groups need to be small enough that everyone can contribute. Third, the task students work together on must be clearly defined. The cooperative and collaborative learning techniques presented here should help make this possible for teachers. Also, in cooperative learning small groups provide a place where:
- Learners actively participate;
- Teachers become learners at times, and learners sometimes teach;
- Respect is given to every member;
- Projects and questions interest and challenge students;
- Diversity is celebrated, and all contributions are valued;
- Students learn skills for resolving conflicts when they arise;
- Members draw from their past experience and knowledge;

- Goals arc clcarly identified and used as a guide;
- Research tools such as Internet access are made available;
- Students are interested in their own learning.

History and development of cooperative learning
Prior to World War II, social theorists such as Watson, Shaw, and Mead began establishing cooperative learning theory after finding that group work was more effective and efficient in quantity, quality, and overall productivity when compared to working alone. However, it wasn't until 1937 when researchers May and Doob found that people who cooperate and work together to achieve shared goals, were more successful in attaining outcomes, than those who strove independently to complete the same goals. Furthermore, they found that independent achievers had a greater likelihood of displaying competitive behaviours.

Philosophers and psychologists in the 1930s and 1940s such as John Dewey, Kurt Lewin, and Morton Deutsh also influenced the cooperative learning theory practised today. Dewey believed it was important that students develop knowledge and social skills that could be used outside of the classroom, and in the democratic society. This theory portrays students as active recipients of knowledge by discussing information and answers in groups, engaging in the learning process together

211

rather than being passive receivers of information (e.g., teacher talking, students listening).

Lewin's contributions to cooperative learning were based on the ideas of establishing relationships between group members in order to successfully carry out and achieve the learning goal. Deutsh's contribution to cooperative learning was positive social interdependence, the idea that the student is responsible for contributing to group knowledge.

Since then, David and Roger Johnson have been actively contributing to the cooperative learning theory. In 1975, they identified that cooperative learning promoted mutual liking, better communication, high acceptance and support, as well as demonstrated an increase in a variety of thinking strategies among individuals in the group. Students who showed to be more competitive lacked in their interaction and trust with others, as well as in their emotional involvement with other students.

In 1994 Johnson and Johnson published the 5 elements (positive interdependence, individual accountability, face-to-face interaction, social skills, and processing) essential for effective group learning, achievement, and higher-order social, personal and cognitive skills (e.g., problem solving, reasoning, decision-making, planning, organizing, and reflecting).

Advantages of Co-operative Teaching Method

Celebration of Diversified Idea
Students learn to work with all types of people.
During small-group interactions, they find many
opportunities to reflect upon and reply to the diverse
responses fellow learners bring to the questions
raised. Small groups also allow students to add their
perspectives to an issue based on their cultural
differences. This exchange inevitably, helps students
to understand other cultures and points of view.

Acknowledgment of individual differences
When questions are raised, different students will
have a variety of responses. Each of these can help
the group treated a product that reflects a wide
range of perspectives and is thus more complete and
comprehensive

Interpersonal development
Students learn to relate to their peers and other
learners as they work together in group enterprises.
This can be especially helpful for students who have
difficulty with social skills. They can benefit from
structured interactions with others. Cooperative
learning requires students to learn to work together,
which is an important skill for their futures. They
develop their interpersonal skills and they learn to
deal with conflict. In small groups, students can
share strengths and also develop their weaker skills.

Actively involving students in learning

Cooperative learning is interactive, so students are engaged, active participants in the learning. Each member has opportunities to contribute in small groups. Students are apt to take more ownership of their material and to think critically about related issues when they work as a team.

Better understanding of lessons

When cooperative groups are guided by clear objectives, students engage in numerous activities that improve their understanding of subjects explored.

More opportunities for personal feedback

Because there are more exchanges among students in small groups, your students receive more personal feedback about their ideas and responses. This feedback is often not possible in a large-group instruction, in which one or two students exchange ideas and the rest of the class listen.

Disadvantages of cooperative learning
Same Grades, Unequal Effort

When grading a group work, all members of a group may receive the same grade, this is a disadvantage for members of the group who do a majority of the work. Additionally, when projects such as written reports are graded, it may be difficult for the teacher to determine which parts of the project were completed by each group member. To fight potential inequality, the teacher can carefully monitor groups as they work to determine each member's contribution.

Groups Can Be Overly Social
Cooperative groups can be created by student or teacher selection, and each has some disadvantages. When students are allowed to select their own groups, they may choose based solely on social preference, which may encourage students to stray from the assigned task. On the other hand, if the teacher selects groups, there is a danger of grouping together students of similar abilities, which may create a group of very weak students or grouping students who may not work well together.

Lesson Planning Can Take Longer Time
With students working in groups, the teacher's task in managing the whole classroom is slightly more difficult as the students are required to interact. The teacher will have to design a lesson and assessment ahead of time that is appropriate for group work and allows for the fair evaluation of all students. The teacher will also need to develop a task that will engage all group members for the allotted time. Additionally, teachers need to be extra vigilant about plagiarism in group work, particularly if each member is required to turn in their own final project.

Classroom Management Challenges

While many of cooperative learning's disadvantages affect the students, the strategy can also provide difficulties for educators. For students to work together, they must talk to one another. Any teacher who has managed a classroom of 20 to 30 students knows that when kids are given the permission to converse with one another, invariably the noise level increases, which can become a distraction from the learning process. It is also impossible for one teacher to constantly monitor each group, which can result in off-topic encounter. Students working in groups might also leave their seats to review materials together. Without strict discipline, cooperative learning can reduce an organized classroom to utter chaos.

Mobile Teaching Method (E-Learning)
Origin and Development: The invention of mobile learning technology dates back to1200, when Abacus was invented in China. In 1895 Marconi achieved the 'Hello Wireless' radio transmission device. The development of the first wireless phone by Alden followed in 1906. In 1964, the CDC 6600 (the first) supercomputer was released orchestrating the idea of computing in education in the 18th century. In 1984, Psion Organiser (personal pocket computer) was introduced granting individuals personal access to information. The idea of knowledge —sharing via mobile technology became pronounced in the year 2010 when the Bloom fire iPad was born.

Mobile learning is a pedagogical concept that has been introduced into the educational system from the previous century. It is born out of the E-Learning' concept and involves the use of electronic gadgets like mobile phones, laptops/palmtops, radio e.t.c. M-learning is a learning method employed in the dissemination of educational instruction(s) with assistance of handheld technology. It is ability to obtain or provide educational content on personal pocket devices such as PDAs, smartphones, and mobile phones.

Mobile learning method is the use of any mobile or wireless device for learning on the move, It is any service or instructional facility that supplies a learner with general information and education content that aids their acquisition of knowledge regardless of location and time (Lehner &Nosekabel, 2002).

It is an educational approach which encourages flexibility and offers students to participate in learning irrespective of age, gender, membership of any specific group or geography. It eliminates the issue of space, time or place that could traditionally constitute a barrier or obstacle to education or literacy (provided electronic wave [Network] is available). This is why Vavoula & Sharple (2002) in Kinshuk (2003) opines that learning can be considered mobile in terms of space, area of life and with respect to time. Sharple (2000) defines mobile learning as the "knowledge and skills" people need to prosper throughout their lifetime. This teaching method enables students to become adaptable to flexible and contextual life-long learning and fulfils the basic requirement needed to support such life-long learning experiences by virtue of its high degree of portability, unobstructive nature and adaptability to the context of learning and the learners evolving skill and knowledge (Sharple, 2000). According to Kinshuk (2003), mobile learning facilitates provision for educational opportunities.

Types of Mobile Learning
Woodard (2011) enumerated the following as the different types of mobile learning
- SMS communication
- MMS (Multi-media messaging service) containing text massages and graphics
- WAP (which helps mobile phones to access the internet through deploying protocol of international standard)
- PDA (Personal Digital Assistance) device function work like PC compatible machines, Palm OS or PC Ma OS
- Bluetooth
- MP3 file format
- PDACAMs

Mobile Learning in Distance and Nomadic Education
Distance learning and nomadic education are instances of mobile learning method. Distance learning is an important aspect of non-formal

education that caters for those who lack access to the traditional, bricks and mortar, or the four-walls of classroom to learn. It is a mobile learning technology supported by ICT to provide significant learning opportunities for formal and non-formal continuing literacy in adults and youths educational programmes. It takes learning beyond the traditional or formal education programmes for adults by means of computer skills and 'digital literacy' often defined as a given program of learning objectives.

Through mass media and correspondence this form of education creates possible access to health education, civic education, literacy (as in the Open Universities /Correspondence Courses) and vocational training. Radio and Television programs have been introduced to improve literacy especially in rural areas for this purpose. Distance and nomadic learning approach attaches relevance to the nomadic populace whose nomadic life-style prevents or hinders their participation in the normal / conventional school system.

Highly populated countries like China, Cuba, Mexico and Nigeria are the countries that have adopted the combination of Distance learning and ICTs approaches in the education of their citizens - having proved that the method does work. Below is a chart showing the nomadic groups in Nigeria.

Nomadic Groups Distribution in Nigeria

S/NO	GROUP	POPULATION	LOCATION
1	The Fulani	5.3m	Northern Nigerian Pastoral nomads
2	The Shuwa	1.0m	Northern Nigerian Pastoral nomads
3	The Buduman	35, 00	Northern Nigerian Pastoral nomads
4	The Kwayam	20,000	Northern Nigerian Pastoral nomads
5	The Badawi	Exact number not yet known	Northern Nigerian Pastoral nomads
6	The Fishermen	2.8m	Rivers, Ondo, Edo, Delta, Cross River Akwa-Ibom State, and Bayelsa State

Source: Table showing the six nomadic groups in Nigeria as the year, 2000 (FME -Education Sector Analysis, 2000)

Mobile Learning Theories

Some theories employed in the distance or online education for mass literacy majorly includes motivational learning theory, cognitive learning theory and constructivist learning theory as the curriculum may spell. In the distance education of the nomads particularly, the motivational (which encourages and heightens cooperative learning among learners) and cognitive learning theories (that enhances learners ability to cooperatively partake in dialogues and interaction which helps them to grasp the conceptual learning material) are more appropriate and can easily be achieved when electronic literacy programmes are displayed or relayed in local languages.

Mobile Learning Strategies

Instructional techniques like radio and television stories, drama, special educational programs like the traditional! conventional literacy class sessions, Quiz, Debates, political/civic and religious issues, Health Talks, industrial programs (like wood works, food processing and arts e.t.c.), Safety Education e.t.c. offers what could be described as multi-media pedagogy.

Mobile Schools

Mobile schools use collapsible classroom that can be assembled or disassembled within thirty minutes and carried conveniently by pack animals. A typical mobile unit is said to consist of three classrooms able to serve the capacity of fifteen to twenty children. Some of the classes are also equipped with audio-visual materials.

Characteristics of Mobile Learning

Kinshuk (2003) spelt out the following as the characteristics of mobile learning:

Urgency of learning needs

Initiative of learning acquisition

Interactivity of learning setting
Situatedness of instructional activities
Integration of Instructional Content

Although, mobile learning activities are not confined to a specified time or space, Kinshuk further suggested that it should be capable of delivering educational contents to learners at anytime and anywhere they need it.

Advantages
- ❖ It is learner-centred
- ❖ It is an easy way to access lessons
- ❖ It makes learning very flexible
- ❖ It grants access to Online Learning Communities
- ❖ It encourages interaction with fellow learners and the lesson facilitators or instructors
- ❖ It grants access to complete instructional information and improves retention
- ❖ The portability of PDA devices enables students to note and gather any type of data very easily
- ❖ Owning personal mobile devices motivates and heightens student's commitment to use and learn with them. Access to instructional contents and data is neither limited by time and space.
- ❖ It enables students to learn at their own pace

- ❖ It reduces the cost in the acquisition of learning materials and computation expenses.
- ❖ It has no geographical boundaries.

Disadvantages
- ❖ Storage-capacity of devices is limited
- ❖ Battery life span is very short.
- ❖ It is difficult to develop some contents sometimes because of unavailability of a common platform
- ❖ Some software or devices soon turn out to be obsolete
- ❖ Where there is no network connection, it becomes difficult to use devices. Distribution of concrete instructional materials requires the visitation of local coordinators or supervisors
- ❖ Adult learning cannot be conducted solely through this media strategy (in Nigeria) because the method is used to primarily support the conventional education program.
- ❖ The use of ICT/distance learning method has immediate resource constraints or challenges for the professional development of literacy facilitators than for the literacy programs themselves.

Factors that Influence the Choice of Teaching Methods

In the selection of teaching methods the teacher should consider the following factors. Keziah and Ajoku (2003) identified the following factors.

- ❖ Lesson objectives
- ❖ The subject
- ❖ Class size
- ❖ Equipment available
- ❖ Time available
- ❖ The best way to present the subject
- ❖ Group knowledge of the subject
- ❖ The kind of participation anticipated by the teacher

To Uwalt (2006), the following factors should be considered in the choice of teaching method.

- ❖ Specific learning objectives
- ❖ The learner
- ❖ Subject matter
- ❖ Resource materials
- ❖ Class space
- ❖ Comfort of the learning environment
- ❖ Time

A brief discussion of these factors are made below

- ❖ **Specific Learning Objectives**

  Every instructional process is centred on the statement of objectives commonly called specific objectives. The content of the specific objectives to a large extent, determine the direction of the lesson. For example, if the

224

objectives reflects critical thinking and judgment, the teacher cannot embark on narrative as a teaching method, rather the teacher in this regard should adopt expository method.

❖ **The Learner**
In contemporary instructional process emphasis is on the learner rather than the teacher. This calls for the much acclaimed learner centred approaches that have occupied the centre stage of many education literatures. The learner in this regard includes his interest, age, motivation, norm, background, gender and other variables. For example, the play-way method of teaching is more adopted for use at the pre-primary and primary school level than the lecture method because of the developmental characteristics of the learner.

❖ **Subject Matter**
Different subject matters demand different things relative to the activities of the teacher and the student. Some subjects such as the sciences and technology are practical-oriented while some are theoretical, abstract or narrative in nature. For example, a teacher teaching topics on Introductory Technology, Practical Biology, Chemistry or Physics is

more likely to adopt the activity method than another teacher teaching topics on History, Bible Knowledge or Social Studies. This is because most topics in the sciences as stated above use more a practical approach than those of History, Bible Knowledge or Social Studies.

❖ **Resource Materials**
The uses and application of instructional materials in the teaching learning process cannot be overemphasized. Instructional materials in this context, means the resources used by the teacher in the teaching learning process aimed at achieving the objectives of the lesson. In any situation, the presence or availability of resource materials affect the choice of teaching methods. For example, a teacher who finds himself in a classroom environment where instructional materials are well provided will be motivated to use them. By so doing, he may adopt the activity, experimental or expository method of teaching.

❖ **Class Space**
The classroom space to a large extent serves as a determining factor that influences the choice of teaching methods or strategies in most public schools in Nigeria (mostly in the urban centres) are over populated ranging from the ratio of 1/100 students, one teacher

226

to one hundred students. In some situation the students are compelled to study in deprived learning environment. In a situation such as this, the teacher cannot perform wonders, the teacher in this regard has to choose methods that suits the class population and the general learning environment, which may be the lecture, discussion or story- telling method of teaching.

❖ **Comfort of the Learning Environment**
Learning environment in this regards means the atmosphere in which teaching and learning takes place. It includes variables such as the class space, lighting, ventilation, furniture, and some other physical facilities. It also includes psychological learning environment such as school rules and regulations, leadership styles, communication channels, administrative procedure and other motivational variables. In a comfortable learning environment, the teacher will be motivated to use appropriate teaching methods that will promote or enhance learning.

❖ **Time**
Time at teachers disposal determines the selection of teaching methods by the teacher. Time in this regard should be examined on two perspectives. The first has to do with

duration; which implies how long the lesson will last in relation to the time allocated on the timetable. In this regard, the teacher is expected to fashion the learning activities to suit the time. The second is the period of the day. For example, it will be unprofessional to carryout physical education activities during the afternoon period. Subjects like mathematics that require critical thinking are always taught in the early hours of the day than the afternoon.

Summary and Conclusion
This chapter has examined the concept of instructional method and the various teaching methods that can be used in our school system. In the assessment of teaching methods, the chapter classifies it into three, such as the teacher centred methods, learner centred methods and innovation teaching. Lastly, the chapter emphasizes on some factors that teachers need to consider in the choice of teaching methods and conclude that teaching methods are not used indiscriminately that teachers should consider certain factors in its application for effective instructional delivery.

CHAPTER SEVEN

INSTRUCTIONAL MATERIALS IN TEACHING

Introduction

The uses and application of instructional materials is an important component of the teaching/learning process, which the student teacher needs to be well informed about. In this regard therefore, this chapter focuses on the concept of instructional materials, classification of instructional materials, the advantages and disadvantages of instructional materials, in relation to the teaching/learning process.

Concept of Instructional Materials

Various terms have been used for instructional materials. Some call it curriculum materials, apparatus, teaching aids, educational media, instructional media and even educational technology. Whatever be the case, instructional materials relate to the concrete object used in the classroom by the teacher and the students in the teaching/learning process. Mkpa (1987) defines instructional materials as aids or resources, which the teacher and in fact, the entire class utilize for the purpose of making teaching/learning more effective. Gbamanja (2001) opines that instructional materials refer to those resources, which appeal to all senses and enrich learning. Such materials include; chalkboard, visual symbols, still pictures, models, motion pictures, photographs, radio, television, programmed materials, textbooks and other print materials. Jeremiah (2009) sees instructional materials as anything used by the teacher to satisfy the educational need of the learner. He further states that instructional materials are the resources (material) used by the teacher in the teaching/learning process with the primary aim of achieving the objectives of the lesson.

Classification of Instructional Materials
Instructional materials can be classified according to different criteria.

The two basic ones are: according to how they appeal, to the various senses and according to the mode of usage.

According to How they Appeal to the Senses
The three categories of instructional materials in this classification include visual aids, audio aids and audio-visual aids.

Visual Aids:
They are those teaching/learning aids that appeal to the sense of sight or vision. Such materials include display boards, printed materials of all types, specimen, models and pictorial materials.

Audio Aids: They include instructional materials that appeal to the sense of hearing i.e. the ear.

Examples of such materials include audiotapes, telephone, radio sets, megaphone, talking book or album, computer and handset.

Audio-Visual Aids:
They are those teaching aids that appeal to both the sense of sight and hearing at the same time. Examples of such teaching aids includes television set, computer sound film, cinema, video materials and internet.

According to Mode of Usage
The three categories of instructional materials that fall under this group include: Non-project materials, projected materials and project motion pictures.

Non-Project Material:
These are materials which do not require extra power before they are presented during teaching and learning. Examples include: diorama, pictorial materials, printed materials, display board, charts models, maps and posters.

Projected Materials:
These groups of instructional materials stand still when they are projected until they are removed. Examples include slides, filmstrip and associated transparencies, opaque projector and microscopic projectors.

Project Motion Pictures:
These moves in their natural form when they were filmed. An example is sound films with their associated projectors, the 88m and 16mm film projectors.

Uses of Some Specific Teaching Aids
Chalkboard:
This is one of the oldest teaching aids available in education, which can effectively be utilized by the teacher. Owing to its simplicity of construction, the chalkboard is readily available in every classroom and immediately ready for use by the teacher with skill developed through practice, and understanding, it can be utilized effectively for certain types of communications with a group in a class situation. It is quick and easily assessable means of putting down words or drawing and simple line or diagrams during a lesson or discussion. The symbol can be quickly written or erased and new materials added to meet the changing requirement of students. The major types of chalkboard the student teacher may come across include wall blackboard, pulley or roller chalkboard, magnetic chalkboard and the easel chalkboard and more recently, the interactive board.

How to use the Chalkboard
The teacher should position himself only on one side of the board while writing or illustrating an idea;

Use vertical lines and divide the chalkboard into two or more parts before using or writing on the board;

Do not talk to the chalkboard while teaching;

The teacher should use duster not hand in erasing any information on the chalkboard;

Use pointer not finger to point out any information or illustration on the board;

Writing on the chalkboard should be bold and legible;

Drawing and other illustrations on the board should be clear.

Specimen:
These are the real materials or the actual teaching aids the teacher utilizes in the class. It can be specimen of insect, chemicals, animals, plants etc. The use of specimen makes teaching to be real to real life situation. In science, specimen can be used in teaching of lesson on plants, animals, skeleton, to mention but a few.

Models:
Models are three dimensional teaching aids that can be rated second to specimen. Models are representation of real objects i.e. it is used when the teacher cannot provide the real object in the class. For example, a model of snake, scorpion or even

skeleton can be provided by the teacher when he wants to teach topics related to them. One important feature of models is that children can handle, observe, smell and even play with them so much that they offer a more realistic approach to teaching than mere description. In another view, the construction of models provides an excellent opportunity for participation by the pupils on individual or group basis. Thus models are representation of real objects. Models can effectively be used by the teacher in the teaching of a vast array of subjects in science, technology, arts and even social sciences.

Wall Charts and Poster:
In the order in which they appeal to pupils' sense, wall chart and posters come next to models, and as a result of the ease with which they can be made or because they can simply be bought. Teachers in Nigeria make more use of them than either models or even specimen. At this point the authors have to sound clearly that not all commercially produced charts are adequate for teaching, because according to Bello (1981), most of them are too crowded and confused. Thus the authors advice all teachers to produce their own charts showing just those information they need for each lesson or series of lessons.

Qualities of a Good Chart

a. The chart must be simple in details not complicated so that it is clear and not confusing;

b. The lettering for its heading should be one inch in height so that it can be read with ease by all children in the class. Other lettering within the chart can be smaller if so desired;

c. All words in the chart should be horizontal and not diagonal, so that the children do not have to turn their heads sideways before reading the words;

d. Appropriate colour should be used in the chart to make it look more attractive.

Pictures:

Where it is not possible for the teacher to get specimen or models for illustration, he could then use pictures. Specifically, coloured ones add a lot of meaning to teaching and save the teacher lengthy descriptions, but the effective use of pictures demands that the teacher should know the appropriate stage at which he should introduce the picture in the course of his lesson presentation. The right selection of any other media that, if combined with the pictures would further help clarity and understanding of a point or points that need stressing. These other media possible for combining with the use of picture include verbal explanation, dramatization, play-back of recorded passages or explanation. It is important to note that no matter how good a picture may be, if introduced to the class

235

at the wrong time, may fail to produce the desired effect in the learner.

Sources of Obtaining Pictures:

The student teacher can obtain pictures from the following:

Periodicals such as magazines, newspapers, pamphlets;

Posters, charts and photographs of different places such as markets, banks, parks, landscape;

Pictures on topics relating to foreign countries can also be obtained from the embassy or consulate offices in the country; Annual calendars of companies and government also form another useful source of picture collection. Most of their pictures are both educational and colourful.

Maps, Atlases and Globes:

Maps have an added advantage over both picture and charts in that they present something real and at the same time do so in the form of a summary. Every map is a symbolized summary of real thing and the information it shows is very condensed and thus requires close study. Therefore, the best type of map that can be introduced to small children is the very large scale survey map, which shows only a small location. Atlases are available for Geography, History and Religious Studies. There importance lies on the fact that they allow private individual study by the children. The purpose of Globes is to show the true relationship between land and seas and the earth's surface; like maps, globes, if introduced too early can lead to number of misconception.

Importance of Instructional Materials
The following are some educational values of instructional materials
   - ❖ They make learning more permanent;
   - ❖ They supply a concrete basis for conceptual thinking and reduce meaningless words responses of pupils;
   - ❖ They have a high degree of interest for the learner;
   - ❖ They develop a continuity of thoughts; this is especially true of motion pictures;
   - ❖ They contribute to growth of meaning and hence, to vocabulary development;
   - ❖ Teaching aids arouse curiosity, stimulate imagination and enlarge viewpoints.

Suggested Guidelines for the use of Instructional Materials
The following guidelines are suggested for a teacher to consider in the use of instructional materials:
   - ❖ The instructional materials whether imported or locally made, must
      suit the age level and experience of the learners;
   - ❖ The materials must make learning more real and meaningful to the learner;
   - ❖ The student teacher must have good knowledge of the material;

- ❖ The student teacher should also consider the cost of producing' the instructional materials
- ❖ The instructional materials should be relevant to the subject, topic and above all objectives of the lesson;
- ❖ The instructional material should be the one that is readily available to both teacher and the student;
- ❖ The accommodation of the material within the lesson period should also be considered;
- ❖ The instructional materials should be portable and not too complex for learner to understand.

Summary and Conclusion

In this chapter, we have examined the concept of instructional materials and its classification. The chapter in its analysis of the concept of instructional materials also explained in simple terms the uses and application of some instructional materials and teaching aids as it provides a guide to the teacher on optimum utilization of such resources. Importance of instructional materials as it relates to the teaching/learning situation was also highlighted. The chapter therefore provides a systematic guideline for the use of instructional materials and concludes that in any teaching/learning process, the must be important instructional materials to be used as specimen, followed by model, picture or chart.

CHAPTER EIGHT

EVALUATING INSTRUCTIONAL OUTCOME

Introduction
Evaluation of instructional outcome is a very important component of the teaching/learning process. As such, every trained teacher needs to have a good knowledge about it. In this regard, this chapter examines the concept of evaluation, types of test, grading system and above all continuous assessment procedure.

Concept of Evaluation
The concept of evaluation has been defined by scholars in different ways. It can be likened to the description of the elephant by the six blind men of Hindustani. In contemporary times, three models of evaluation have evolved on which the various definitions of the concept revolve.

The classical conception of evaluation is the one of passing judgment, thus it has been defined as judging the worth of an entity, experience, idea or a purpose. On the other hand, evaluation also involves the process of passing judgment with regard to the value of a given entity based on certain criteria. Viewing it from the angle of instruction, evaluation can as well be defined as the systematic process of determining the extent to which specific objectives are achieved.

Hence, the focus of any evaluation is to determine the congruence between performance and objectives. Alkin (1970) opines that evaluation is the process of ascertaining the decision area of concern, selecting appropriate information, collecting and analyzing information in order to report summary data useful to decision makers in selecting among alternatives. Evaluation asks such questions as how good? How effective? How adequate? How satisfactory? etc. Evaluation therefore, is primarily aimed at interpreting measured performance in the light of certain criteria. The outcome of such interpretation is expressed in quantitative terms as: pass, failed, excellent, good, bad, satisfactory, worthless and successful.

Types of Evaluation
We have two major types of evaluation viz:

Formative Evaluation
This type of evaluation is undertaken at the early stage of an instructional programme. It is carried out periodically while instruction is still in progress. Through this type of evaluation, information is obtained which is used to make necessary modifications in the instructional process. The major purpose of formative evaluation is to provide regular or periodic feedback, which can be used to improve the effectiveness of teaching learning

process or the curriculum, in general. It provides information on the strength and weakness of the student's learning as well as those aspects of the instructional technique and materials that are not adequate. Such information is then used in making necessary modifications in the instructional technique and materials to help students overcome their areas of weakness. Class work, home work, weekly text, quizzes, teacher's observation or rating are all forms of formative evaluation.

Summative Evaluation
This type of evaluation is carried out at the end of a course of instruction to determine what an individual has gained or acquired from the course. The evaluation may be at the end of a unit, a course, term, year or period of schooling. The main purpose is to determine what an individual was able to acquire at the end of the unit, course, term, year or period of schooling. It is usually a one- short business, which comes at the end of the course. Hence, by the time information is obtained, it is not possible to make any modifications in the course. Examples of summative evaluation include: the First School Leaving Certificate Examination, Junior School Certificate Examination, Senior School Certificate Examination, Teacher Grade II Certificate Examination to mention but a few. It is important to note that the different between formative and summative evaluation is very tenuous. In same situations formative evaluation can be used summatively while in some other situation

241

summative evaluation can be used formatively. (Akpe, 1999).

Types of Test

A test can be defined as a systematic procedure for observing a person's behaviour, and describing it with the aid of numerical scale or category system. Also, a test is a device or instrument for obtaining a sample of pupil's behaviour. It is normally made up of tasks, questions, and situation intended to elicit particular type of behaviour. The major types of test examined in this work are objective and essay tests.

Objective Test

The objective test items are highly structured questions that limit the type of response the testee can make in order to provide answer to the test. Objective test question is drawn in a way that irrespective of who scores it, the score of the testee remains the same. Hence, the major issue on objective test item is the scoring. It has a pre-determined answer, which the testee either selects or supplies. The major types of objective test Include: supply answer test, true or false test, matching test and multiple choice items.

Supply Answer Test: In this type of objective test, the task of the testee is presented in a sentence in which a word, a phrase, a number or a symbol is omitted. The testee is expected to complete the sentence by supplying a response that provides a complete knowledge for a blank or a series of answers for a series of blanks.

Examples of Supply Answer Test
1. Nigeria gained her independence in the year
   _____
2. _____ was the first executive president of Nigeria
3. The process by which plants manufacture their food is known as

True or false Test:
This type of objective test is presented as a declarative statement in which the testee is expected to make decision as to its truthfulness or otherwise. After making the decision, the testee marks 'true' if the statement is essentially true or 'false' if the statement is essentially false. Other forms of alternative response are yes or no, correct or incorrect, agree or disagree, right or wrong and the like. The major problem with this type of test is that it encourages guesswork.

Examples of True or False Test
Port Harcourt is the capital of Rivers State. True or False

Animals with backbone are called vertebrate. True or False

The most popular Jihad in Western Sudan was carried out by Usman Dan Fodlo. True or False

243

Matching Test:

This type consists of two parallel columns. In one column, there are words, numbers or sentences which are to be matched with words, symbols or phrases in the other column. The item in the column which seeks the matching are called premises, while the item in the column from Which the selection is made is called responses. The testee is instructed to make an association or connection between pairs of element. Matching item are useful in measuring pupils ability to associate, relate, or interpret element or events learnt in the classroom. It is an effective test instrument for nursery and junior primary school level mostly when pictures and illustration are involved.

Examples of Matching Test

Column A	Column B
Farmer	Stethoscope
Carpenter	Fuel
Tailor	Hoe
Driver	Hammer
Doctor	Tape

Multiple Choice Items:

A multiple choice item, consists of a problem and suggested solution from which the testee selects a response. The problem may be direct question or incomplete statement called stems The lists of response; are known as alternatives. One Of, the alternatives is keyed as correct response by the examiner (but not known to the testee) and the pupil is asked to read the stem and select the correct or best alternative. In this regard, the correct alternative is called answer. While the other alternatives are referred to as detractors because they are deliberately constructed wrongly, to a student who does not achieve the desired objective being measured by the item.

Examples of Multiple Choice Items
_____ was the father of Abraham. (a) Terah (b) Jonah (c) Lot (d) Ahab
Animals that feed on plants are called _____. (a) Mammals
(b) Carnivorous (c) Herbivorous (d) Terrestrial
The largest desert in African is _____. (a) Sahara
(b) Kalahari (c) Sanhel (d) Sudan

Advantages of Objective Test
Scoring objective test response is very objective because different scores will arrive at the same scores for each response.

It is useful for testing pupils at the junior levels of our primary school who do not have much writing skills to express themselves as in the cases of essay test.

It ensures content validity of the test because the instructional content is more adequately sampled.

It makes the testee to read extensively, as the questions are often drawn from the topics covered.

Scoring the objective test item does not require a special skill.

The pupils hand writing and other variables cannot affect scoring or reduce or inflate the measure of demonstrated achievement because correct responses are either provided or known.

Disadvantages of Objective Test
It is not very effective for measuring higher mental or intellectual processes.

If the test is not properly administered, the testee can cheat thereby encouraging examination malpractice.

Objective tests are very difficult to construct.

Sometimes objective test encourages guesswork mostly the alternate response and the matching test.

It does not give the testee the opportunity to organize and present ideas in his own way.

Essay Test
The essay test is also called free answer test. It is a type of test in which responses are presented in the form of continuous and connected writing and the testee is free to express himself in a series of

arranged sentences. Hence, the testee supplies the responses himself. Also there is no precise limit to the length of the responses to be provided. We have two major types of essay test, which are extended and short answer test.

Advantages of Essay Test

It can be used to analyze and evaluate written expression and organization of ideas mostly when extended-response item is used.

It provides the testee the opportunity to develop writing skills.

Essay test is easier to construct.

It offers the maximum freedom of response to pupils, which can be used to assess higher cognitive behaviour such as analysis, synthesis and evaluation.

It allows the examiner to test the testee's opinion without making pre-judgments on the opinion as it is with the selected-response items. Here, it is the pupils ability to defend an opinion that is assessed rather than assessing the pupils agreement with keyed opinion.

Essay test enhances the assessments of speed, quality and writing.

Disadvantages of Essay Test

Extraneous variables such as hand writing, speed which may be irrelevant to the intended objects of the test may affect testee's score either positively or negatively.

There is the problem of comparability of performance mostly when the testee does not attempt the same question.

It is difficult to establish exact time limit for each questions.

It makes more time to score than the case of objective test.

It has a low scorer reliability.

Scoring and Grading System in Tests

Scoring simply means assigning scores or numerals to testee performance in a test so as to determine their levels of performance. Related to scoring is grading which similarly means assigning grades to pupils performance in test to determine the level or degree of performance. There are different ways of scoring and grading which are discussed below:

A Simple Raw Score:

Any score awarded to a question, part of a question or questions are called a raw score. The simple raw score is used everyday by the teachers in our schools. If for example, a child scores 6 questions, his raw score is 6 out of 10 possibilities (6/10). The problem with raw score is that, it does not show the child's performance in relation to other children's performance. Its advantage is that, it is easy to apply as a method of scoring.

Percentage Score: This is expression of raw score in percentage (%). It is calculated by placing the child score over the maximum possible score and multiplied by 100. For example, if the child's raw score is 6 out of 10 as, indicated above, his percentage score is calculated thus

$$\frac{6}{10} \quad X \quad \frac{100}{1} \quad = 60\%$$

Letter Grading:
This involves the use of letters, i.e. alphabet to represent grades made by the testee in a test. Letter grades are based on percentage of correct scores. Although the grading system varies from one institution to another, the trend follows the example below, which is a six-point scale:

Grade %	Interpretation	Points
A -70 & above	Very Good	5
B – 60-69	Good	4
C - 50 - 59	Average	3
D – 45-49	Poor	2
E – 40-44	Very Poor	1
F - 39 & below	Failure	0

Note:
The advantage of this system of grading is that 100 marks have been compressed into six grades, which can be used to measure the relative performance of a testee in relation to others in the class. The major disadvantage of letter grading is that the range is too wide e.g. 60 69 (B).

Simple Ranking
This involves the placing of testee's score in order of merit such that the testee with the highest grade score takes the first position, the next highest score takes the second position and the testee with the lowest score takes the last position. A simple ranking score is presented below.

Table1: **Simple Ranking Score 1**
In a situation where two or more pupils have scored the same marks, the most common method is to assign the same mark rank to all that have the same marks using the next lowest rank in the group. For instance in the table below,: pupils 4, 6, and 7 should occupy position three, four, and five, but position three should be assigned to them the next pupil with the next highest score is assigned rank 6 skipping rank 4 and 5.

Simple Ranking Score I

S/N	PUPILS	SCORE	RANKING
1	Emeka Ogarabe	85	2nd
2	Chukwuchebe Ohia	61	6th
3	Mary Peterson	72	4th
4	Blessing Silk	55	7th
5	Anyawu Ekutus	43	8th
6	Dorcas Omoime	68	5th
7	Kelvin Humphrey	98	1st
8	Divine Onwuka	77	3rd

Simple Ranking Score II

S/N	PUPILS	SCORE	RANKING
1	Ahamefula Ohia	62	7
2	John Mattew	55	8
3	MmaAtasia	82	2
4	Mercy Ahaiuzu	75	3
5	Onisogin Kanikwum	70	6
6	Minebaze Ezekiel	75	3
7	Chukwuka Jeremiah	75	3
8	Guzzo Ohia	88	1

Continuous Assessment in Teaching

In the past, assessment of pupils in our school system was examination centred and as well based only on one short examination. Many educators have observed that this system assessed only the cognitive domain to the complete neglect of the affective and psychomotor. Although passing statement were made as to the character of the pupil but such was not based on any objective assessment.

This system caused a lot of problem in the educational system. In order to redress these problems, the National Policy on Education (2004) introduced an innovative assessment procedure called continuous assessment. According to the handbook on continuous assessment (1980), the concept is defined as a mechanism whereby the final grading of a student in the cognitive, affective and psychomotor domain behaviour systematically takes into consideration all his performances during a period of schooling. Fulanjo and Orerinde (1984) define continuous assessment as the mode of evaluation that takes into consideration all the experiences and achievements of the pupils throughout their school career. Also, continuous assessment can be defined as a way of identifying what a student has learnt during a given period of schooling.

Characteristics of Continuous Assessment
The various characteristics of continuous assessment are discussed below:

ContinuousAssessment is Systematic;
This quality of continuous assessment indicates that it requires an operational plan that indicates what measurement to be made and what type of instrument to be used in assessing the learner.

Continuous Assessment is Comprehensive:
This characteristic explains that the types of instruments used to assess the child are many. Such instruments may include inventory, observation, test, project, questionnaires, checklist, sociometric technique and anecdotal records.

Continuous Assessment is Cumulative:
This is because the decision to be made at any time about the learner takes into account all the previous decisions about the learner. This involves the keeping of all records about the pupils.

Continuous Assessment is Guidance Oriented:
This indicates that the information obtained about the pupils is used to guide and direct his future development.

Advantages of Continuous Assessment
❖ The result of assessments are used for guidance purposes.
❖ All domains are taken care of during assessment.
❖ Assessment is coordinated. It is not haphazard.

- ❖ The learner does not lose anything on transferring from one school to another. There is a common assessment plan, so results of assessment for the individual learner can be transferred from one school to another.
- ❖ Under continuous assessment, learner's deficiencies are identified and remedied immediately.
- ❖ Assessment is made part of teaching. In continuous assessment, feedback from school assessment is used to improve classroom teaching. This is made possible as assessment goes hand in hand with teaching.
- ❖ In continuous assessment, teachers are actively involved in the evaluation process.
- ❖ The use of continuous assessment helps to reduce the threat syndrome that one short test examination poses.

Disadvantages of Continuous Assessment
- ❖ It takes too much time of the teacher.
- ❖ Lack of materials such as calculators, filing cabinet and stationery
- ❖ Poor record keeping
- ❖ It may be abused by an unpatriotic teacher.
- ❖ Truancy of pupils, and failure to turn in assignment.

Summary and Conclusion

This chapter has examined the concept of evaluation relative to the various types of evaluation used in our school system. This chapter also looked at the various types of test, mode of construction and their advantages and setback. The issue of scoring and grading system was also discussed with a view of educating our teachers the best model of grading our students for a proper and objective assessment of students instructional outcome.

Lastly, the issue of continuous assessment was also discussed, with its attendance characteristics. The chapter therefore concludes that instructional evaluation is a key factor in the teaching/learning process as such teachers should be well-informed of the mode of evaluation in order to enhance objectivity in the assessment procedure of students in the class.

REFERENCES

Aderinoye, R. A. (2005). Innovation in Mass Literacy Promotion in Nigeria: the introduction of Cuban Radio Literacy Model. 2005 ICDE International Conference, November 19-23. New Delhi India.

Aderinoye, R. A, ojokheta, K.O., Alojede, A.A (2007). The internal review ofintegrating mobile learning into nomadic program in: Issues andperspectives:

http://www.irrodl.org/index.php/irrod/article /view/ 347/919
Retrieved March. 25, 2017.

Afongideh, M.E. (2009). *Curriculum Implementation at the Basic Education Level.* In U.M.O. Ivonietal(Eds.) Curriculum Theory & Practice (pp 168 — 179). Curriculum Organization of Nigeria.

Akinkpelu, J.A. (1981). *An Introduction to Philosophy of Education.* London: MacMillan Press.

Amajirionwu, S.A. (1985). *Set Induction.*In R.O. Ohuche& L.U.NIzuwah (Ed.) Microteaching Effectiveness. Onitsha: Summer Education Publishers.

Ausubel, D.P. (1963). *The Psychology of Meaningful Verbal Learning.* New York: Ginue and Straton.

Barrows, Howard S. (1996). 'Problem-based learning in medicine and beyond: A brief overview" .new Directions for Teaching and Learning. 1996 (68): 3-12. doi: 10. 1007/tI.37219966804

Bergmann, J., & Sams, A. (2012).*Flip your classroom: reach every student in every class every day. Washington, DC:* International Society for Technology in Education. https ://en.wikipedia. org/wikiplipped_classroom

Biodun, O. (2009). *Some Key Concept for Understanding Curriculum.inIvowi, U. M . N. et al (Ed) Curriculum Theory and Practice. Curriculum Organization of Nigeria (CON) pp 1- 20.*

Brunner, J. (1961). *The Act of Disoveiy: Harverd Educational Review* 31(1)21- 32. V

Brunner, J. (1990). *Act of Meaning. Cambridge. M.A: Harverd University Press.*

Deroay, J. (1933). *How We Think.*Boston D.C. Health.

Emerwa, H.N. (1981). *"Factors In Curriculum Planning"in U. Owuwuka (ed). Curriculum Development in Africa. Onitsha*: African FEP publisher.

Etuk, G.K. & Afangide, M.E. (2008). *Curriculum Organization arid Change.*Ugo: Scholars Press.

Federal Government of Nigeria (1989).NCNE Decree 41 of 2. December 1989. Lagos

Federal Republic of Nigeria (2004).*National Poilcy on Education.* Lagos: Federal Ministry of Education Press.

FRN (2004).National Policy on Education. Lagos: Federal Ministry of Education Press.

Gbamanja, S.P.T. (2001). *Essentials of Curriculum and Instruction.* Ado Ekiti: AlaPampns Ltd.

Gbamanja, S.P.T. (2005).*Essentials of Curriculum and Instruction.* Ado Ekiti: AlaPempus Press.

Gbamanja, S.P.T. (2014). *Science Education and Economic Development of African State.*World Educators Forum (3 — 1) 20 — 36.

Gilles, R.M., & Adrian, F. (2003). Cooperative Learning: The social and intellectual

Outcomes of Learning in Groups. London: Farmer Press. http://!www.thirteen.org/edoniine/concept2cla sslcoopcollab/https ://en.wikipedia.org/wiki/cooperative learning.

Ibe-Bassey, G.S. (2002). *The Teacher and the Instructional Process*. A paper presented at the World Teachers Day Celeberation in AkwaIbom on October 7th 2002.

Jayme Jenkins (2016). Learning Industry: http://elearnih.com/6-mobile-learning-   benefits-mobile learning-revolution

Jeremiah, S. (2004) *Summative Evaluation of Basic Science Curriculum in Primary Schools in Rivers State*. Unpublished M.Ed Thesis, Rivers State University of Science and Technology, Port-Harcourt.

Jeremiah, S. and Alamina, J.I. (2006) *Fundamental Principles of Curriculum Process and Planning Owerri: Career Publishers*

Jeremiah, S. (2009) *Principles and Methods of Teaching.*Owerri: Joe Mankpa Publishers.

Jeremiah, S. (2010) *Instructional Strategies and Pupils Achievement and Retention in Primary Science.Unpublished Ph.D* Thesis, University of Uyo, Akwa-Ibom State, Nigeria

Jeremiah, S. & Job, G. (2011).*Micro Teaching at a Glance.Owerri:*JeoMankpa Publishers.

Jeremiah, S. (2013).*Lesson Planning and Lesson Presentation in Teaching Practice.* A paper presented at the Teaching Practice Orientation Programme Organized by Federal College of Education (Technical), Omoku, Rivers State.

Johnson, M.C. (1967). *"Definitions and Models in Curriculum Theory"* Educational Theory 17(2)127-140.

Johnson, D., Johnson, R. (1975). Learning together and alone, cooperation, competition, and individualization. Englewood

Johnson, D., Johnson, R. (1994). Learning together and alone, cooperative, competitive, and individualistic learning. Needham Heights, MA: Prentice-Hall.

Jonasseb, D.H. (1999). Constructing learning environments on the web: Engaging students in meaningful learning.EdTech 99: Educational Technology conference and exhibition 1999: Thinking Schools, Learning Nation

Keziah, E. &Ajoku, N. (2003) *Fundamental of Curriculum Development and Implementation.*Owerri: Pen Publishers.

Keziah, A.A. (2007). *Microteaching, A Practice for Teaching Skills. Port Harcourt:* Pearl Publishers.

King Alison. "From sage on the stage to guide on the side."College teaching 41 1: 30-35.

Kinshuk (2003). Adaptive mobile learning technology. Department of Information Systems: Massey University, New Zealand. Retrieved May 19 2007 from: hhtp://www.Whirligig .com .au/globaleducators/articles/kinshuk2003.pdf

Laffey J., Tupper, T., Musser, D., &Wedman, J (1997). A computer-mediated support system for project based learning. Paper presented at the annual conference of the American Educational Research Association, Chicago, IL

Maureen Lage, Glenn Platt, Michael Treglia (2000), Inverting the Classroom: A gateway to Creating an Inclusive Learning Environment, Journal of Economic Education.

May, M. and Doob, L. (1937). Cooperation and Competition. New York: Social Sciences Research Council

Miles, M. B. (1973). *Educational Innovation: The Nature of the Problem in Miles (ed) Innovation in Education.* New York: Teachers College Press.

Mkpa, M.A. &Izuagba, A.C. (2012).*Curriculum Studies and Innovation.* Owerri: Mercy Divine Publishers.

M kpa, M .A. (1987).*Curriculum Development and Instruction.Owerri:* Totan Publishers.

Novac, J.D. (1990) *Concept Maps and Vee diagrams.Truo Metacognitive Tool for Science and Mathematics Education.*Instructional Science 19, 29 -52.

Nworgu, B.A. (1998) *Constructivism a New Trend in Primary Science Teaching.* A paper presented at the Annual Workshop for Primary School Teachers organized by Imo State Primary Education Board.

National Teachers Institute (2009). *Curriculum Model on PDE 104 Curriculum Design & Development.* Kaduna: NTI Press.

Nwafor, O. (2007). Educational Innovations: Process and Product.Enugu: Magret Business Enterprises Publishers.

Offorma, G.C. (1994). *Curriculum Implementation & Instruction*.Onitsha: Uni World Publishers.

Offorma, G.C. (2005).*Curriculum Implementation for Functionality*.J Oriafor, S.O., Edozie, G.C. &Ezeh, D.N. (Eds) Curriculum Issus in Contemporary Education (pp 107 — 203) Benin City.Dia Silvia Influences.

Offorma, G.C. (2006). A Lead Paper on Curriculum Issues in the 21st Century. Journal of Curriculum Organization of Nigeria (CaIa bar Chapter) 2(1)26 -39.

Okoroma, N. S (2017) Policy Sumersaults in Education: A National Delima. 44th Inaugural Lecture Presented at the Rivers State University, Nkpolu – Oroworukwo, Port Harcourt.

Onyiye, A.O. & Olawoye, A.S. (2008).*Female Students PercelevedCauses and Solution to Examination Malpractice in Asa Local Government: Implication forCounselllng*.www.unilorin.edu.ng/publicatio n/eniye/femalestudentsperceived (droniye). Htm August

Oteh, I.E. and Akama, N. (2010).*Curriculum Development and Innovation.* Aba: Eagle &Joy Publishers.

Parker, j. Palmer (1997) in Constructivist teaching methods:
http://en .m. Wikiped ia.org/wiki/constructivist_teaching_method

Pring, R. (1972).*Curriculum Philosophy and Design.*Welton Hall, Briston: The Open University Press.

Saylor, J.G.; Alexander, W.M. & Lewis, A.J. (1981). *Curriculum Planning for Better Teaching and Learning.*

Singh, Y.K. (2008). *Teaching Social Studies* NewDelhi: APH Publishers.
Sharan, Y. (2010). Cooperative Learning for Academic and Social Gains: valued pedagogy, problematic practice. European Journal of Education, 45,(2), 300-3 13.

Sund, Robert B. &Tworobridge, LW. (1973). *Teaching Science by Inquiry in the Secondary School 2nd Ed. Charles E. Merril Publishing Company.*

Tanner, D. &Tanner, L.N. (1975).*Curriculum Development: Theory into Practice.* New York: Macmillan Publishing Co.

Todd, R.W. (1965). *Curriculum Development and Instructional Planning.* Nederland, TX: Nederland School District.

Thirteen Ed Online (2004).Constructivism as a paradigm for teaching and learning.http;//www.thirteen.org/endoline/concept2class/constructivism/index. Html

Unruh, G.C. & Alexander, W.M. (1974).*Innovation in Secondary Education (2nd Edition).* New York: Halit, Rinebert and Winston Inc.

Vavoula, G.N. & Sharples M (2002). Kleos: A personal mobile knowledge and learning organisation system. In Millard, H.U Hoppe and Kinshuk (Eds.) IEEE Internal Workshop on wireless and mobile techniques on Education (page 152- 156) Los Alamitos, CA.IEEE Computer

Witrock, M.C. (1977). *Learning and Instruction. (Reading in Educational Research Series).* –

Wood D, (2003). "ABC of learning and teaching in medicine: problem based learning ". British Medical Journal. 326:328-330. dio: 1136/bmj.326.7384.328

Wood, & Middleton, (1975).A study of assisted problem solving. British Journal of Psychology, 66(2), 81-191.

INDEX

www.ingramcontent.com/pod-product-compliance
Lightning Source LLC
LaVergne TN
LVHW051225080426
835513LV00016B/1409